WHEN THE SUBJECT IS RAPE

A GUIDE FOR MALE PARTNERS, FRIENDS & FAMILY MEMBERS

Alan W. McEvoy, PhD

SQUAREONE
PUBLISHERS

The information and advice contained in this book are based upon the research and the personal and professional experiences of the author. They are not intended as a substitute for consulting with a healthcare professional. The publisher and author are not responsible for any adverse effects or consequences resulting from the use of any of the suggestions, preparations, or procedures discussed in this book. All matters pertaining to your physical health should be supervised by a healthcare professional. It is a sign of wisdom, not cowardice, to seek a second or third opinion.

Typesetting and cover design: Gary A. Rosenberg

Square One Publishers
115 Herricks Road
Garden City Park, NY 11040
(516) 535-2010 • (877) 900-BOOK
www.squareonepublishers.com

Library of Congress Cataloging-in-Publication Data
Names: McEvoy, Alan W., author.
Title: When the subject is rape : a guide for male partners, friends &
     family members / Alan W. McEvoy.
Description: Garden City Park, NY : Square One Publishers, [2023] |
     Includes index.
Identifiers: LCCN 2022060482 (print) | LCCN 2022060483 (ebook) |
     ISBN 9780757005220 (paperback) | ISBN 9780757055225 (ebook)
Subjects: LCSH: Rape. | Rape—Psychological aspects. | Rape victims—
     Family relationships. | Man-woman relationships—Psychological aspects. |
     Interpersonal relations—Psychological aspects.
Classification: LCC HV6558 .M334 2023 (print) | LCC HV6558 (ebook) |
     DDC 364.15/32—dc23/eng/20230106
LC record available at https://lccn.loc.gov/2022060482
LC ebook record available at https://lccn.loc.gov/2022060483

Printed in the United States of America

10   9   8   7   6   5   4   3   2   1

Contents

Acknowledgments, vii

Preface, ix

Introduction, 1

1. Understanding Rape-Induced Trauma, 7

2. The Immediate Consequences of Rape, 19

3. Communicating with the Victim and Others, 37

4. Understanding the Long-Term Effects of Rape, 51

5. The Impact of Rape on Sexual Intimacy, 65

6. Parental Concerns During the Recovery Process, 81

7. Non-Stranger Sexual Assault, 93

8. Working with Law Enforcement, 105

9. Rape as a Hate Crime, 121

10. Post-Traumatic Growth, 133

Conclusion, 141

Resources, 144

About the Author, 151

Index, 153

To the Rose
who endured anguish beyond measure
yet never ceased to blossom.

Acknowledgments

I am grateful for the encouragement of my daughter Katy and my son Kyle, whose love remains a constant in my life. I am also grateful to Rudy Shur and Square One Publishers for smoothing out the rough edges of this book. Finally, I wish to acknowledge my mentor and friend Edsel Erickson, who has passed from this earth but whose memory endures in his legacy of "passing it forward."

Preface

This book has its origins in an experience I had as a young man in my early twenties—an experience that made me realize how ill-prepared I was to deal with the subject of sexual violence and its complexities. A close friend had the courage to tell me she had been raped. It was an act of trust on her part and, I think, an implied request for understanding. The rape had altered the trajectory of her life, at least temporarily, and she was struggling to make sense of what a man had done to her. She also was trying to regain a sense of control and move forward. At that point, she simply needed a friend to listen to her.

My friend's revelation made me realize that, due to my having grown up as a male, I had neither the framework nor the vocabulary to process what had happened to her or guide my response to her disclosure. I wanted to help but had no idea what to do. My good intentions collided with my ignorance. Neither I nor my male friends had ever had a serious discussion about sexual violence toward girls and women. At no point during my time in high school or college had I honestly considered the topic of rape. I had never reflected on the consequences of rape for women. I had never considered how a man could help a woman who has been the victim of sexual assault. Later I learned just how many men, when confronted with the rape of a loved one, also required guidance.

Throughout my career as a social scientist, I have examined the impacts that various forms of violence can have on people's lives and the ways in which these people might be helped to overcome them. I have found that violence can pose unique challenges for its victims and those who love them depending on the circumstances in which it is expressed, whether these circumstances involve child abuse, intimate partner violence, self-harm, bullying, rape, or some other traumatic event. I have researched and written about such violence as part of my academic work. In doing so, I have realized the need for this information to reach a broader, nonacademic audience—the everyday people who are desperate to know the best ways to help their loved ones to forge a path through the trauma of sexual assault.

As part of my work on rape, I have listened to the accounts of countless people whose lives have been upended by sexual violence. I am grateful to the many women who have spoken openly with me about how their relationships with the men in their lives have been affected by rape, even if the assault had happened years before. I am grateful for the honest disclosures from men whose daughters, spouses, sisters, intimate partners, or close friends have been sexually assaulted. These good men wanted to do the right thing. They understood the devastation sexual assault had inflicted on their loved ones, but many also felt frustrated—even angry—as a result of their ineffective efforts to help them. Some acknowledged that they had said or done things in their efforts that had only strained their relationships with these women. The wisdom I have gained from the women and men who have shared their insights on the subject of rape and sexual assault with me over the years serves as the basis of this book.

This book embraces the idea that men can acquire an empathetic understanding of the complexities of rape and its recovery process. It believes that men will be able to approach this subject from the perspective of women who have been raped if given proper guidance. While aimed at a male audience, this text provides information that anyone whose life has been affected by sexual assault would find invaluable. No matter who reads this book, its guidelines will be most effective if they are followed with patience, sympathy, kindness, understanding, trust, nonjudgment, and love.

When the Subject Is Rape addresses not only the trauma of rape but also the healing and growth that can occur during the process of recovery. It offers not only practical guidance but also hope that light can emerge from such darkness. If a woman you care for has been raped, this book will help you to help her. If you wish to be a true ally in her recovery, then this book is in the right hands.

Introduction

I f a woman or girl with whom you have a close relationship were raped, as a man, would you know how to respond? Would you know how to help her, or would you keep your distance, fearful that you might inadvertently do more harm than good? Even if the rape happened years before, how might this event affect that person and your relationship now? Is there anything you can do to help her to get through this terrible experience? Understanding your role in the situation can be crucial in her moving forward. The experience may have left her with psychological trauma in connection with males in general, negatively impacting her relationships with all the men in her life, including you. How you respond to her behavior and her needs can make a big difference in both her recovery and your relationship.

Sexual violence can be a defining moment in a victim's life—creating a sense of life before the assault and life after. The trauma of rape ripples outward in concentric circles of harm, starting with the victim and extending to others with whom she is connected. For victims and those who love them, rape can give rise to what feels like a major shift in the ground upon which they have built their lives. Things once taken for granted, such as feeling safe or being able to manage daily routines, are no longer so. In addition, problems that existed prior to the event are now amplified. As a man who cares for someone who has been raped, you may feel a sense of uncertainty. This sense of uncertainty likely stems from two basic questions: What can I do to help, and what effects will this event have on her, me, and our relationship?

Most rape crisis centers and counseling services focus on providing direct help to victims, and most counselors and victim advocates who help women who have been raped are women. Most men have very little experience in dealing with the consequences of rape, and few are likely to know what to say or how to behave in support of victims. As this book will show, however, men who are close to a rape victim can have an enormous impact on her recovery—whether positive or negative—depending on what they say or do. Men who are in a position to help a female loved one in her recovery from sexual assault need guidance to address this issue properly.

THE CHALLENGE FOR MEN

Given that the majority of rapes involve male perpetrators and female targets, generally men do not see themselves as potential victims. Men do not live with the fear of rape and, as a result, lack an adequate understanding of sexual violence and its consequences. It is not that men are indifferent to the safety concerns of teens and women. Rather, the daily precautions taken and apprehensions shared by females who grow up in a climate in which rape is an ever-present possibility are simply absent, for the most part, from the male mindset.

Although approximately one out of five women will experience sexual violence in her lifetime, the deficiency of knowledge on this subject among men is disheartening. Seldom is the topic of rape included in educational discussions in school or the media. In addition, most males have not had honest and open conversations with women, or with other men, about the reality of sexual violence, nor have they discussed its profound effects on women. It is no wonder why so few men are prepared to help when a woman they love is sexually assaulted.

The first step men can take is to learn the basic vocabulary necessary to discuss sexual violence. Legally speaking, *rape* involves any vaginal, oral, or anal penetration (including with objects) without the victim's consent. Force or threat of force, coercion, or manipulation may be included in some statutory language, but the essential element in rape is lack of consent. *Sexual assault* is a more inclusive term and generally refers to a wider range of attempted or actual unwanted sexual contact between offenders and victims. Both are expressions of sexual violence. In everyday speech, however, the terms often are used interchangeably, as they are in this book.

Think of rape as a criminal act of violence that is expressed sexually. It includes the brutal imposition of a perpetrator's will on a person who is not able to resist. Rape is also a form of emotional and physical terrorism in which violent sexuality overpowers and dehumanizes a victim. In the most basic sense, rape violates a victim's body, mind, and spirit. Rape is about power, control, humiliation, and domination expressed in a sexual act. Many victims are physically brutalized, terrorized with threats of bodily harm or death, and frightened into silence. This means rape is a life-threatening and life-altering experience that shakes a victim to her very core.

Experts in the field use terms such as *victim* or *survivor* in reference to someone who has been raped. Both terms are acceptable, though each conveys a somewhat different meaning. Within the context of the criminal justice system, a *victim* is a person who is the target of a crime and who has rights under the law. Although some people believe the word "victim" carries negative social stigma, it expresses no judgment of blame, responsibility for the crime, or weakness. A victim in this sense is one who suffers serious injury at the hands of another; it means something harmful was done to a person against that person's will.

The term *survivor*, on the other hand, conveys a feeling of empowerment and strength, and a sense that the victim has reclaimed her life to some degree. Rape survivors, therefore, may be characterized as those who are in the process of recovery or who have achieved some degree of recovery. Survivors acknowledge the harm done to them but have gained perspective and perhaps no longer define themselves as victims. This book focuses on the needs of female victims of rape who are on the road to becoming survivors.

HOW MEN CAN HELP

The goal of this book is to give men the knowledge and skills to help female loved ones recover from rape. Who we are as humans is defined by the quality of our relationships with others and our capacity to make choices for ourselves. Rape undermines the bonds that connect people to each other and removes a victim's sense of self-reliance—the sense that she can choose to act for herself and not be acted upon against her will. Although this book is not meant to replace professional counseling, it provides men with recommendations on how to help female loved ones who have been victims of rape to restore these bonds and regain a sense of control over their lives.

This book draws upon the experiences of women struggling to recover from rape, and the experiences of the men in their lives who endeavor to help in this recovery. At the center of this book is a basic idea: Men who are husbands, fathers, brothers, intimate partners, or friends of women can and do influence how they recover from the trauma of rape. This book offers practical guidance to men about what they should or should not do if a woman they love has been the target of a sex crime. Equally important, it can help in the preservation of relationships that otherwise might deteriorate in the aftermath of rape. Its goal is to teach men how to be a positive influence on a woman's recovery from rape.

WHAT TO EXPECT FROM THIS BOOK

This book might be seen as a roadmap of the complexities of rape and the process of recovery. It provides insights regarding things you should and should not do if someone you love is raped, and it strives to empower you to be an effective ally in a victim's recovery. Among the topics it covers are the following:

- The nature of rape trauma, including the effects of trauma on a person's emotions and memory.

- What to expect in the immediate aftermath of rape, including how to respond to disclosures of sexual violence.

- How to communicate with victims and others following rape, including what to do when victims refuse to talk about what happened.

- The short-term and long-term consequences of rape for victims and those close to victims.

- Fears and concerns regarding the resumption of sexual intimacy for partners of rape victims.

- How to respond when victims and perpetrators know each other, including how to navigate the complexities of rape on college campuses.

- Strategies for working with law enforcement, victim services, and the judicial system.

- Guidelines for parents whose daughters have been victims of sexual violence.

- Special cases of sexual assault such as multiperpetrator rape, interracial rape, and the rape of gender nonconforming or LGBTQIA+ individuals.

- Post-traumatic growth.

This book gives you the tools necessary to help a female friend or relative get through the anguish caused by sexual violence and maintain healthy relationships with you and others. But remember this: Because no two recoveries are identical in the aftermath of rape, there can be no "one size fits all" set of instructions. The path of a teen or adult woman's recovery from rape is multifaceted and rarely, if ever, straightforward. It contains false starts, setbacks, conflicts, and frustrations, but she can overcome these difficult hurdles on her way to recovery with the right support. A victim's journey toward healing from rape is both an individual and a shared one.

Finally, it is important to note that the information found in this book can be put to good use only if it is shared with patience, sympathy, kindness, understanding, steadfastness, trust, nonjudgment, and love. Always keep this in mind.

1.

Understanding Rape-Induced Trauma

Rape is a traumatic event that can affect all aspects of a woman's life, including those relationships most significant to her. Although a full clinical analysis of trauma is beyond the scope of this book, as a support person you should know that there can be enormous variation in how individuals are affected by sexual assault. Whatever the common features associated with rape-induced trauma, no two victims will necessarily respond in the same way to this form of trauma or follow identical paths to recovery. The goal of this chapter is to help you, as a support person, to develop an understanding of the trauma experienced by a woman who has been raped. Your capacity to comprehend her world following the assault will set the stage for you to be an effective ally in her recovery.

PSYCHOLOGICAL EFFECTS

Rape-induced trauma can dramatically alter the ways in which a rape victim lives her life. It can shape how she sees herself, how she thinks others see her, how she interacts with family and friends, how she expresses her emotions, her beliefs about the kind of world in which she lives, and the choices she makes. The need to make sense of what happened and integrate this experience into other dimensions of her life is a common struggle. Such trauma can consume a significant amount of the victim's psychological and emotional energy.

For some, trauma produces what therapists call *dissociation*, which may be described as a feeling of disconnection from one's own emotions, thoughts, or even identity. For example, individuals suffering from *post-traumatic stress disorder,* or *PTSD,* (see the inset "Symptoms of PTSD" on page 10), including rape victims, may enter what is known as a *fugue state,* an extreme form of dissociation in which they lose time for a period (minutes or longer) and seem confused about who they are. Their thoughts and emotions are disconnected from their surroundings, almost as if they are having a vivid dream. They then seem unable to explain where they were or what they experienced during that lost time once they have come out of this state.

For others, there are brief but vivid flashbacks. A person may become overwhelmed by an image or recollection of a terrifying moment that intrudes unexpectedly and leaves the individual feeling an anguished loss of control. Combat veterans, children growing up in war zones, war refugees, victims of violent crimes such as rape, and even victims of natural disasters commonly report experiencing intense flashbacks centered on moments of horror. Often a person does not know what triggers such flashbacks, which can strike like thunderbolts even during routine activities. Given the unpredictability of when a flashback might happen, it is difficult to integrate this intense experience into other aspects of one's daily life. The intrusive flash of memory stands as a separate and frightening aspect of being disconnected from whatever is going on in the moment.

Victims of rape need to know that symptoms such as psychological numbness, feelings of having lost time, and brief but intense flashbacks are common and expected features of trauma. In time, and with proper support, these symptoms tend to subside. It helps victims to learn that such episodes can be a regular aspect of trauma and do not mean they are becoming mentally unbalanced. It also helps if victims feel they are in a safe space where they can talk about what it is like for them to go through such episodes. As a support person, one of your tasks is to help to create that safe space for her, so she can talk about what she endured, if she chooses to do so, without fear of judgment or blame. The ability to talk about a terrible experience is the first step toward recovery.

Although traumatic events are consequential, it is important to understand that they do not define a person. A person who goes through a traumatic incident is far more than that experience alone. It is import-ant to know that trauma need not be perpetually debilitating or function as a permanently handicapping experience. Resilience often surfaces in the face of terrible events. Trauma can be overcome, and with proper support it can even become a means toward continued personal growth. An important step in creating a supportive environment for healing is to understand two things that are likely to surface after a rape: memory problems related to trauma and a sense of isolation. Both unfold within a complex array of emotions experienced by the rape victim.

EMOTIONS AND MEMORY

The aftershocks of rape-induced trauma often include difficult emotions such as anger, fear, shame, guilt, humiliation, helplessness, anxiety, abandonment, grief, resentment, and feelings of injustice. Like the prongs of a fork, the strong emotions commonly experienced by rape victims are connected to a common stem: a sense of having been profoundly tarnished or defiled. It is understandable why many victims develop a deep sense of isolation in the aftermath of rape—they feel that no one can truly understand what they are going through.

One of the most significant outcomes of trauma—one that is especially upsetting to victims—is the emergence of trauma-related memory issues and feelings of confusion in trying to remember the event. This outcome may occur even in the absence of other symptoms of PTSD. Human memory, particularly in connection with traumatic events, is not like a digital file, where every detail is recorded exactly as it happened. A person's memory will be affected when subjected to a combination intense fear, a feeling of powerlessness, and an experience so horrible that it defies words. The act of remembering something traumatic is not straightforward, but rather a journey through an emotional labyrinth. In her book *Survivor Café*, author Elizabeth Rosner points out this seeming contradiction when she asks, "How does atrocity defy memory and simultaneously demand to be remembered?"

An atrocity such as rape has a way of etching itself on a victim's psyche. It lingers in the memory and echoes in the mind. Even if a person tries not to recollect them, some memories of terror appear involuntarily, intruding on everyday thoughts like a flash of light in a darkened room that allows you to catch a glimpse of what's happening within. Other memories may be retrieved voluntarily and often are connected to waves of emotion, including fear. And some experiences of terror are so fragmented that they cannot easily be recalled in a way that creates a complete picture.

Symptoms of PTSD

When confronted with the traumatic aftershocks of rape, most women will initially exhibit negative reactions that gradually dissipate. Some, however, may become symptomatic in ways described by the clinical literature as post-traumatic stress disorder, or PTSD. It is the persistence of these symptoms over time that defines PTSD. Although not all women who have been raped suffer from PTSD, some do. For a diagnosis of PTSD, symptoms must persist for at least one month or longer and include a combination of the following:

- Sleep disruptions or nightmares related to the event

- Loss of appetite

- Mood swings or emotional outbursts with little or no provocation

- Chronic depression, persistent sadness, or an inability to feel happiness

- Loss of interest in formerly pleasurable activities

- Difficulty concentrating

- Lack of motivation

- Avoidance of reminders of the traumatic experience (e.g., people, places, activities)

- Hypervigilance, persistent anxiety over one's safety, or an exaggerated startle response

- Flashbacks or intrusive images

- Memory problems regarding what happened

- Feelings of isolation or negative feelings about the world

- Engaging in reckless behaviors, acts of self-harm, or suicidal ideation

It is important to note that these psychological reactions emerge in response (some would argue a normal response) to frightening experiences. It also is important to understand that such symptoms of PTSD usually fade over time with the proper support, even if memories of what happened may endure.

Memory problems stemming from trauma may be worsened if a victim was under the influence of alcohol or drugs at the time of the assault. In some victims' memories, trauma can distort the timing of events, with recollections not necessarily appearing in their proper sequence. Certain details of an assault may be particularly important to a victim, regardless of the sequence in which they unfolded. Furthermore, some moments of an assault may be remembered with clarity, while others are broken off from full conscious awareness, perhaps only to surface when something unexpectedly triggers their recollection. The main point is that it is not reasonable to expect victims of trauma to recount all the details of what happened in chronological sequence.

In addition, often when people recall traumatic experiences, some things that stand out in their memories may strike others as trivial or even odd. After experiencing a traumatic event, it is common for a survivor to fixate on some aspect of the event that may seem unusual or illogical, even to the survivor. For example, one survivor who was brutally attacked in her father's automobile told this author that during the assault she kept worrying about whether the car might be damaged. Another survivor talked about the gold chain with a crucifix her assailant wore around his neck, which kept striking her in the face as he raped her. Simply stated, as a traumatic event unfolds, certain sights, sounds, smells, or other stimuli can take precedence in a victim's memory. As the ally of a rape victim, it is important to listen and offer no judgment when she offers an account of what occurred, no matter what is revealed. Remember that it is normal for some details of an assault to take on greater weight than others in a victim's memory.

Another possibility to consider is past traumatic events becoming linked in a victim's mind to a new traumatic event. Recollections of prior terrible experiences, including instances long forgotten or never fully processed, may bubble to the surface in the wake of a recent trauma. This tends to happen among victims of multiple traumas, including those who were targets of physical or sexual abuse during childhood or adolescence. A new traumatic experience triggers flashes of previous trauma, thus adding to the victim's distress. A rape victim may not have ever disclosed these prior traumatic occurrences, which have now become significant again. Having become linked in flashes of memory, both sets of events need to be processed on her journey to recovery. As her support person, do not be surprised if she divulges other troubling events in her life, which are likely clues to that which she is processing.

How Trauma Can Influence Memory

There are two especially important things for you to understand about the relationship between trauma and memory. First, recollection of a traumatic event such as rape is likely to unfold gradually, in pieces, rather than all at once in the emotionally charged atmosphere immediately following the incident. When new details emerge over time, it is a serious mistake to assume that the victim was not telling the full truth before, or perhaps was intentionally withholding important facts. Expect that the narrative of what happened will evolve over time and change in some details as the victim gains more distance from the event.

Second, you can neither force people to remember nor compel them to discuss what they wish to forget. Some experiences may never be fully remembered or forgotten. Some memories will remain unspoken, even if they continue to whisper in the background of a person's thoughts. With your love and support, a victim of rape-induced trauma may find the courage and the words to speak of memories that seem unspeakable. Understand that your role is not to interrogate or constantly push her for more details, especially if she does not wish to discuss what happened. Your job is simply to be there for support. (For more information on how to communicate with a victim of sexual assault, see Chapter 3 on page 37.)

It is an act of trust for someone to share a traumatic experience, and it is that person's choice alone to decide the circumstances under which such a discussion will occur. As a sexual assault victim who sees you as a trusted person in her life, she may choose to share some or all her traumatic experience with you. She may also want to protect you from feeling overwhelmed by the knowledge of what happened to her and therefore decide to remain silent. Again, as her ally in recovery, your job is to be supportive in her decisions. In your role as a caring witness to her story or to her silence, you will communicate the critical message that she is not alone.

Understanding the Feeling of Isolation

As a support person, try to place yourself in the position of the rape victim and ask yourself the following questions: What would it be like if you were removed from your familiar surroundings and placed in circumstances where the rules that governed your life in the past no longer applied? What if everyone in your new surroundings seemed unable to understand you? What if many people you encountered appeared to judge you unfairly? What would it be like if you felt unable to trust others? How would you feel if your most intimate and positive connections with others were disrupted by an event that was brutally imposed upon you? If you knew with certainty that you had to live with a truth that few could comprehend, how alone would you feel, and how would you cope?

A profound sense of isolation—of being alone in a world where no one seems to understand—is a common feeling among people who have endured extreme trauma. Although the intensity and duration of feeling isolated will vary from person to person, this sense of disconnection often runs through the lives of those who have intimate experience with trauma, including victims of torture, child abuse, domestic assault, or rape, and even some combat veterans. Understanding this psychological isolation is necessary for anyone who wants to help a person who has been raped.

Rape can change the trajectory of a person's life. For a woman who is raped, nearly all the foundations that hold her world in place may shift. The "old normal" will no longer apply. She will confront the task of finding a "new normal" in which she can reclaim her place in the world. In the process, she will likely feel cut adrift from the moorings she once took for granted. In the wake of such a senseless injustice, she must confront the unknown and struggle with the question: What next?

As a support person, it is important to know that one of the strategies employed by rapists is to say and do things that reduce the likelihood that their victims will speak about what was done to them. The more perpetrators create fear and degrade and dehumanize their targets, the less willing their victims may be to reveal the explicit details of what transpired. Equally important, perpetrators often sow doubt and confusion in their victims' minds by claiming that what happened was consensual, not an assault. This attempt to manipulate a victim by getting her to question her own judgment is known as *gaslighting*.

The silence of rape victims has two outcomes. It minimizes the risk of legal or other consequences for rapists and isolates victims from family, friends, and others who could help them. It is little wonder that rape victims may experience a sense of being separated and "different" from others— different even from the people they were before the assault. This feeling of isolation is compounded by a general lack of public awareness about the situations in which sexual violence occurs and the consequences faced by rape survivors.

EXAMPLES OF SEXUAL VIOLENCE

Rape can occur in a wide range of circumstances, each of which shapes how victims and others understand and judge what happened. The degree to which others may blame or stigmatize the victim, the degree to which perpetrators of rape are held responsible, the nature and quality of victim services, the actions of law enforcement, and the extent to which victims blame themselves can hinge on the way sexual violence unfolds. Examples of sexual violence include:

- non-stranger sexual assault, in which the perpetrator is known to the victim. This is the most common type of sexual violence and includes what is sometimes called acquaintance rape, date rape, or party rape.

- rape committed by a family member. This also includes stepsiblings and stepparents.

- rape committed by a stranger, possibly in connection with another crime such as robbery. This may also include rape associated with abduction.

- custodial rape in jails, nursing homes, detention centers, hospitals, residential rehabilitation facilities, refugee camps, etc.

- rape in which nonheterosexuals or members of the LGBTQIA+ community are deliberately targeted. This is seen as a hate crime in which perpetrators select victims because of perceived sexual orientation or gender identity. This type of hate crime includes a subset called "corrective rape." For example, a male perpetrator (or gang of male perpetrators) may target a lesbian woman perceived to be a "sexual deviant" in the belief that sexual penetration will "correct" her sexual orientation.

- rape of especially vulnerable persons with physical or developmental disabilities.

- statutory rape, which involves an underage victim (not legally of the age of consent) and an older perpetrator.

- gang rape, which may involve perpetrators and victims of different races or ethnicities.

- revenge rape during military conflict.

- spousal rape.

- sexual coercion of children and adolescents (including pedophilia).

Seldom is the nature of each of these variations of sexual violence described in the media or schools. Understandably, the topic of rape is outside the comfort zones of many. Often it is seen as off limits for any in-depth consideration. This absence of education, however, contributes to the persistence of rape myths that imply victims are to blame for what happened.

Without open and informed conversations about sexual victimization, when an adolescent or adult woman is raped, she may think she is the only person who could possibly understand this terrible experience. It is little wonder that women who are victims of sexual violence often suffer in silence rather than risk confronting what so many fail to comprehend. One may never feel more alone than when surrounded by others who do not understand your experience.

BEHAVIORAL CHANGES

Although it may be surprising, it is common for some women who have been raped to behave in ways that seem contrary to their best interests. First, many refuse to seek help or talk about what happened. It is as if they believe they can make "it" go away if "it" is never discussed. Second, many victims of rape do not choose to seek the assistance of law enforcement. They fear that to involve the police would make their victimization public, which they wish to avoid. Some victims, particularly those who know their perpetrators, refuse to report the crime because they do not want to "get the guy in trouble." Others fail to report because they fear retaliation by their perpetrators or his friends. And some victims refuse to report the crime because they think they will not be believed.

It is also true that victims may misdirect others about what happened or how it affects them. Quite simply, they might deny or minimize the event because they feel profoundly humiliated, or because they worry that they will be blamed for what happened. Victims may remain silent because they do not want to impose their emotional turmoil on family and friends. Although such responses serve to isolate the victim, they are understandable in the context of how our society has approached, or has failed to approach, the subject of rape.

In the end, many women who have been raped simply do not want to discuss the complex feelings associated with something that is such a fundamental violation. Some retreat into silence. Some retreat into alcohol or drugs. Some may push away anyone who wants to help, including the people they love. It is as if these women view offers of help as displays of pity and affirmations of their vulnerability. It is as if they say to themselves, "This is not something anyone can know about. This is not something I want help with or can discuss. This is not anyone's business but my own."

For all these reasons, it is crucial that you understand the complicated ways in which any woman, young or old, may see the world after being raped. Your task is to help create a climate of acceptance in which she feels she can speak about what happened without fear of judgment, despite the misunderstanding of others. Know that she is processing what happened and simultaneously gauging how others respond to her as she does so. Because you love and care for her, because you believe in her and know she is not to blame for what happened, she needs to see you as a pillar of support throughout this ordeal.

THE ROLE OF MEN AS SUPPORT PERSONS

The emotional complications of rape victimization, its impact on a victim's memory, its effects on her feelings of isolation and behavior, and the situations in which rape occurs require supportive male figures in a victim's life to think deeply about how they can help. To be maximally effective, the things men need to do are neither simple nor easy. For one, men need to hold in check what often is a reflexive response when confronted with a problem: the impulse to take charge and be in control. Deeply embedded in the socialization of males in our culture is a desire to act decisively and orchestrate solutions to problems. For men to help traumatized rape survivors and function effectively as support persons, they need to relinquish the urge to take charge. Rape denies women a sense of control over their bodies and their lives. Men need to operate with heightened awareness of how rape survivors struggle to regain that sense of control. When a man tries to take charge of the situation, even out of a desire to help, it disempowers the victim further and actually draws focus away from her getting the kind of support she needs. As a man who wants to help, understand that you are not in charge of her recovery; she is.

Although abandoning the impulse to make decisions for a rape survivor is an important step in learning how to be a support person, more is required. As a man, you still need to be in control of something: your own emotions. One consequence of rape is that it brings to the surface a complex spectrum of vulnerabilities and raw emotions. How might this array of emotions affect interactions with loved ones? How will you reconcile the impulse to speak about how you feel and the need to remain silent about it?

Part of the struggle of maintaining emotional control for men is the challenge of knowing how to name and give voice to feelings. What are sometimes described as "dark emotions" arise when a loved one is raped. Included here can be an internal stew of anger, fear, guilt, revenge fantasies, sadness, shame, depression, and perhaps even a degree of resentment toward the victim. Constant brooding over such feelings or allowing these dark emotions to surface inappropriately in interactions with a rape survivor will interfere with your ability to be a supportive and positive force in her recovery. Your ability to maintain emotional awareness and control will place you in the best position to help her focus on healing.

Because you are on a journey with a rape survivor, it is important for you to embrace patience. It is a mistake to expect that life will "get back to normal" according to an arbitrary timetable. Trust that the amount of psychological trauma caused by the assault will diminish over time as she recovers from it. Your interactions with her should be shaped by your patience and trust in her capacity to heal.

There is one other thing for you to consider in your role as a support person: You must rid yourself of your preconceptions about the relative place rape ranks as a life event for her. Again, the experience of sexual violence can be a significant element in a person's life, but rape does not define a person. A person is more than a horrific experience. As a rape survivor shapes a narrative about the things that were done to her, she begins to integrate the experience into the totality of her being. As a man, you can help shape this narrative in a way that encourages both of you to grow together. It is hopeful to know that a great many women traumatized by sexual violence not only overcome the challenges it imposes upon them, but with support they become stronger and more self-reliant.

CONCLUSION

Traumatic events have a way of shattering a person's sense of self. Victims often feel fragmented and struggle to reassemble the pieces of their lives. They may ask, "Now that this has happened, who am I and what am I to become?" Although more will be said about this idea in Chapter 10 (see page 133), there is a phenomenon called post-traumatic growth that emerges from terrible experiences of loss and pain. Out of her struggle to deal with trauma, she may find a feeling of strength and a sense of resolve that she did not realize were there. She may find new meaning and purpose in life and realize that she has the capacity to define herself anew. Your love for her will facilitate this process. Setting the stage for her healing process begins with how you respond in the immediate aftermath of learning of the rape.

2.

The Immediate Consequences of Rape

The hours and days immediately following the rape of a teenage girl or adult woman are extremely emotionally charged and difficult to navigate for the victim and for those who may know what happened. Not only has she been profoundly violated and terrorized, but the shock waves emanating from the experience confront her with additional worries. Depending on the age of the victim, these worries may first center on a set of questions she is likely to ask herself. (See the inset "Questions in the Aftermath" on page 20.) The questions that linger in her thoughts will have an impact on her recovery, and on her communication with you and others. This chapter focuses on the implications of a critical decision she will face: whether to remain silent or make known what was done to her.

No matter how loving and caring others may be, many rape victims, for a variety of reasons, decide not to tell anyone about the incident, and most do not report the crime to police. (See the inset "Why Some Victims of Rape Remain Silent" on page 30.) It is likely that the relatively young ages of many rape victims may cause them to fear the repercussions of their talking about the rape and thus decide to remain silent. More than 40 percent of rape victims are under the age of eighteen, and about four out of five victims are under the age of thirty. Young women between the ages of sixteen and twenty-four are at highest risk of sexual assault. Even if they decide to talk about the rape, many victims delay telling anyone for a considerable time. This raises a couple of basic questions: If a victim does not divulge what happened, how would you know she was raped? Are there signs that might help an astute observer notice that something is wrong?

Questions in the Aftermath

The physical and emotional trauma experienced by an adolescent or adult victim of rape is compounded by the added stress of a series of questions she is likely to face in the immediate aftermath. The decisions she makes with respect to these questions can set the stage for how she interacts with others in the days that follow. A rape victim will frequently ask herself the following questions:

- Am I safe now?

- Will he attempt to rape me again?

- Do I report this to the police?

- What will the legal consequences be for me and my family if I contact the police?

- Should I seek medical attention?

- Did I contract a sexually transmitted infection, such as syphilis or HIV?

- Am I pregnant?

- Should I tell anyone what happened, and whom can I trust with this information?

- Will anyone believe me?

- If I speak out, will there be retaliation?

- How can I protect my family and friends from the turmoil this will cause?

- What will my family and friends think?

- Will someone I care about demand that I do something I do not want to do?

- Will I be blamed for what happened?

- What should I do if or when others find out what happened?

- How might this affect my sexuality?

- How will this affect those I love?

- How will this affect my ability to perform at work or school?

- Will my life ever again be normal?

IDENTIFYING SIGNS OF DISTRESS

Have you ever been with a family member or close friend—someone you know well and care about—who seemed deeply troubled by something but refused to talk about it? Were you left guessing what the concern may be? Did you say anything? Did you feel upset by this person's silence? Did you assume this person didn't trust you enough to talk about the problem? What were the clues that suggested to you that something was wrong?

Most of us have had such an experience and were not sure what to do to help. When the source of a person's distress is rape, it is important to recognize the signs that point in this direction. If you suspect rape as the source of distress, it is also crucial to understand how to raise your concerns in a way that is helpful.

General Signs

No one particular sign will necessarily indicate the reason for a person's apparent suffering. In addition, because there can be many reasons for a person's distress, overlapping signs can be confusing to interpret. After an adolescent or adult woman has been raped, there may be both general indicators and specific indicators of distress, the combination of which forms a pattern that suggests sexual violence as the cause.

One general indicator of concern is a significant change in a person's emotional state and behavior without apparent reason. This change may include withdrawal from others or being distant and distracted at unusual moments, sleep disturbances, loss of appetite, gastrointestinal disorders, anxiety, hypervigilance, mood swings, an increase in alcohol or drug use, a sudden decline in personal hygiene or disregard for personal appearance, signs of PTSD, depression, self-injury, expressions of guilt and low self-worth, an inability to experience positive emotions, and suicidal ideation or attempts. If such symptoms appear abruptly or out of the blue, they generally indicate that some form of traumatic event has occurred. There are also additional, more specific signs that may suggest that the traumatic event was sexual assault.

Specific Indicators

Some rape victims will respond to touch by recoiling—even to an innocuous touch on the arm or shoulder, or possibly a gentle hug. This reaction is especially noteworthy if the victim has never exhibited such a response in the past. Sometimes the response is so sudden and intense that it seems as if an electric shock has passed through her body as she jumps away involuntarily. If then asked what is wrong, she may offer an explanation that does not seem to fit the circumstances.

Another possible indicator of sexual assault is how she responds to highly sexualized or violent imagery in the media. If she has been raped, such images can cause flashbacks or an unexpectedly intense emotional reaction. She may suddenly burst into tears, abruptly walk away, appear to be lost and disconnected, or exhibit other responses that seem disjointed in this setting. If asked about her response, she may offer an explanation that seems off and perhaps is intended to direct your attention away from the actual cause of her distress.

Another possible indicator that she has been raped may seem paradoxical: Although she has not divulged what happened, she raises conversational themes that center on sexual issues and possibly sexual assault. It may be that she is testing the waters to see how others might respond as she ponders whether to reveal the assault. It may also be she is hinting at things to provoke a discussion about matters that are churning in her thoughts. Younger victims of rape are especially prone to raise such sexualized conversational themes as they process what happened.

Another behavior to look out for is her being suddenly concerned for her own safety in connection with everyday activities. She may fear being alone or going to places where there are other people. If going to school, work, or the store, or for walks, or to see friends—activities that she would normally do without any worry—now seem to cause her paralyzing anxiety, then this could be a clue that her fears are connected to a specific event.

A final set of clues to consider is the presence of physical indicators that might include the appearance of cuts, bruises, swelling, or other signs of injury to her body. Approximately half of sexually assaulted women experience various degrees of injury, although not always in locations that can be observed without a medical examination. Obviously, such physical indicators would only be present immediately after the attack and remain visible for a few days. Beyond this time frame, however, another possible physical condition may remain: an unexplained pregnancy.

Pregnancy is an especially significant indicator of possible rape if the victim is not known to be involved in any consensual intimate relationship. The overwhelming panic experienced by any victim impregnated because of rape (especially a young adolescent who still lives with her parents) creates a terrible dilemma. Whatever moral qualms she may or may not have about terminating the pregnancy, it is highly likely she will seek information about her options. She may begin to ask questions about how to "help a friend" who has an unwanted pregnancy. She may go online to find information on pregnancy options. She may go directly to organizations such as Planned Parenthood or other clinics looking for help. It is also possible she may not know she is pregnant for several months and then must confront the decision about what to do as time grows shorter. Some of the general behavioral indicators of distress previously mentioned can serve as clues that something is amiss.

EXPRESSING CONCERNS

If you observe a pattern of signs that indicate someone you care about is in turmoil, and if you suspect she may have been raped, what is your best course of action? This clearly is difficult territory to navigate if she has not been willing to reveal the reasons for her behavioral changes. That said, is it appropriate for you to share with her your observations and express your concerns for her wellbeing? The answer is a definite yes. Remaining silent despite your suspicions will not remedy her plight. It is *how* you express your concerns that can break her silence and open lines of communication with her. As a person who wants to help, your goal is to find that delicate balance between being supportive and willing to listen, accepting her decisions, and not pressuring her to take a course of action that is contrary to her wishes.

Although more will be said about effective communication with rape victims in the next chapter, it is important and necessary that you risk letting her know what you find worrisome. If she has shown troubling signs of distress but has not offered a credible explanation, look for the right moment to raise your concerns. This conversation is high stakes and likely to be emotionally charged, but it can create an important breakthrough if handled in the proper manner.

Before approaching her, you first need to check your emotions and make certain you are coming from an open, empathic, and loving mindset. If your emotional state is one of resentment or anger at her silence, then wait until you are in a better place before you commit to this conversation. Start the conversation by letting her know you are speaking from the heart and from a place of respect and goodwill toward her. Reassure her that you want to provide a safe space for honest communication without judgment or demands, and that this conversation is not about accusations or making anyone feel guilty. Finally, let her know that this talk is mostly about giving her an opportunity to speak freely, and that your role is primarily to listen.

In a calm manner, honestly state the pattern of things that have concerned you regarding the changes you have observed in her emotional state and behavior. Reassure her that you want to be a positive and supportive force in helping her deal with whatever she is confronting. You can avoid the perception that you are being judgmental by asking her questions such as, "Can you tell me if what I have observed is accurate?" and "Are you willing to tell me what is going on?" Give her a chance to tell her story without interruption. You are not there to interrogate but to listen.

Pay attention not only to what she says but also to how she says it. If she does not want to explain what she is dealing with, you may say, "If you do not wish to talk about this with me just yet, will you let me help you find someone with whom you can talk?" Be careful not to suggest that an unwillingness to discuss matters with you means she does not trust you.

If you strongly suspect she has been raped and she still refuses to talk about what happened, there is one additional thing you may consider. There are national hotlines and local rape crisis centers that receive anonymous calls. (See the Resources on page 145.) A caller is not required to provide a name or contact information. Given the protection of anonymity, it is both appropriate and not a violation of trust for you to make such a call, explain your observations, and ask for resources and professional guidance. At that point, you could explain to her that you made this anonymous call out of concern for her wellbeing, and then present her with the resources you received. It is now her choice whether to act upon this information. Even if she does not respond positively at first, you have created a way for her to seek help when she is ready.

WHAT TO DO WHEN SHE SAYS NOTHING HAPPENED

The question remains: What if she shows unmistakable signs of distress and you have tried everything to encourage her to talk, yet she still refuses? Should you do something to force the issue in the name of helping her? There are several important considerations here to keep in mind.

The Possibility of Self-Harm

If she has given indications that she is considering—or has attempted—suicide or other extremes of self-harm, then you need not ask her permission to act. The immediate danger requires bringing help to mitigate the crisis. The action you take may depend in part on the nature of your relationship with her (as a parent, spouse, or friend). For example, if you are her friend and she still lives with her parents, they should be contacted and told what you know of her behaviors. If you are together in college, you should inform someone from student services that you suspect she may be considering self-harm. The school has experience in dealing with students who are in such a crisis state. If you are her parent or spouse, you should contact local mental health services and ask for help, most likely in the form of an intervention.

What Is an Intervention?

What typically happens in an intervention is a mental health assessment followed by some form of counseling involving a trained professional. An intervention would likely include speaking with her close friends and family members about what they may know, or if she has disclosed something but asked them to keep it a secret. Although the type and duration of counseling will vary depending on the assessment, the goal is to give her the immediate support she needs to lower the risk of self-harm. It is within the context of such crisis counseling that she may reveal the source of her distress, which may be that she has experienced sexual violence. Keep in mind that the need for an intervention in the face of serious risk of self-harm outweighs the possibility of her being angry at you for violating her privacy.

Fear of Retribution

If there is no reason to believe she might hurt herself, her refusal to divulge what happened may be rooted in something truly sinister: her belief that the perpetrator will kill her or seriously harm someone she loves if she talks to anyone about what happened (not just the police). There have been cases in which members of criminal gangs or crime syndicates have made such threats. In addition, the perpetrator may have taken sexually explicit photos or digital recordings of her and threatened to post them if she divulges what happened. Under such a cloud of danger, her refusal to talk about being raped would make sense.

Accepting Denial

You must tread carefully and be open to the possibility there could be understandable reasons for her silence. It may be difficult to accept, but she has the right to make that choice. If you acknowledge to her that you do not understand the reasons for her silence but accept her decision, you will build trust. You still have the option of contacting a counselor or a rape crisis center and asking for guidance and resources, which you can give to her.

WHAT TO DO WHEN SHE TELLS YOU SHE HAS BEEN RAPED

After the initial shock of a sexual assault, many victims do, in fact, decide to talk about what happened with someone they trust. Although she may have been reluctant to talk at first, if you have created a safe space and conveyed your desire to be supportive, there is a good chance she will decide to share her narrative with you. If she is willing, you can help her determine the next steps to take in addressing the many issues in front of her. Acknowledge that you do not have all the answers but are willing to seek solutions with her. With her permission, you may explore some of the following concerns together:

- Does she have personal leave or sick days to take time off from work if needed? Can she be given work to do from home?

- Are there counselors available who have experience working with sexual assault survivors?

- When and under what circumstances should family members and others be told?

- If she decides to report the crime to police, how can you help her during the investigation and legal proceedings?

- Will she want to file a civil suit against the perpetrator? Does she need an attorney?

- Will she want to relocate for safety reasons, and what are her options?

- If things were lost or stolen during the attack, can they be replaced?

- If the case is publicized, what are her rights and protections in terms of the media?

- If she is in school, can she be absent without penalty if necessary? Can she be given work to do from home?

- If the rape occurred in an institutional setting such as a college, do campus officials know? If so, how are they responding to her needs? Can she take time away from school without penalty? Can she secure a refund if she needs to leave school? If there is a case investigation, is she receiving guidance from campus professionals on what to do?

- If she is a minor and in school, what (if anything) should her teachers and school officials be told?

- What should be done if private information about what happened is posted on social media?

- What should be done if someone representing the alleged perpetrator attempts to contact her?

In the questions listed above, there are two that take on critical significance in the aftermath of rape: whether to seek immediate medical attention and whether to report the assault to the police. In the best of all worlds, one might hope that every rape victim would receive medical care directly following the assault and decide that such a violation justifies police involvement. Unfortunately, many rape victims are reluctant on both counts. Because medical and legal procedures may unintentionally contribute to a victim's trauma, the consequences of sexual assault may continue well beyond the attack. Although a full analysis of all the medical and legal procedures is beyond the scope of this book, try to understand her position and consider the reasons for her possible reluctance to secure medical or legal services.

MEDICAL AND LEGAL PROCEDURES

If a victim decides to report her rape to the police immediately, she will be asked not to disturb any evidence until police arrive. In a sense, her body is now a crime scene. She will be taken to a hospital and asked to undergo a medical forensic exam before evidence is destroyed. Her natural impulse, however, may be to shower and scrub certain areas of her body, douche, change her clothes, brush her teeth, and apply medication to any injuries. Yet police and medical professionals will not want her to bathe, brush her teeth, change her clothes, eat, drink, smoke, comb her hair, urinate (if possible), or defecate (if possible) until evidence is collected. Because some biological evidence on her body can deteriorate over time, the earlier the medical forensic exam is taken, the better. Other forms of evidence, however, can remain viable for very long periods, including physical evidence at the crime scene, clothing, foreign objects, and fingerprints. Given advances in technology, DNA from clothing or other objects can be tested even decades after the crime. Such forms of evidence can strengthen the case for prosecution.

The police will also want to gather evidence at the location where the assault took place. She may be asked to accompany the police to this location to retrieve evidence if it is safe to do so. If the suspect poses a danger to the victim or others, the police may have the victim accompany them on a drive-by to identify the address or location. She will be asked to explain to the best of her recollection the sequence of events that occurred, if there were any witnesses, if she was with others before the assault, and if she said anything to anyone after the assault. In effect, she may be asked to recall—in essence, to relive—details of the rape in the location where it transpired. Although these procedures are standard in evidence collection, imagine how emotionally complex they must be for any victim.

Whenever possible, the medical exam should be conducted by professionals trained in working with victims of rape. Ideally, this might include a sexual assault nurse examiner who is part of a sexual assault response team, which is available in many communities. In addition, it is standard procedure to contact a victim advocate from a rape crisis center who can be present during the medical exam and police interviews. Advocates are trained support persons who guide victims through the range of procedures following a sexual assault. The victim has the right to stop the medical exam at any point. She also has the right not to answer police questions, which may be asked if someone else reported the assault. Law enforcement alone has the authority to determine if a suspect should be arrested, and only the prosecutor decides if the suspect should be formally charged.

Although unintentionally so, the medical exam itself may be especially distressing for the victim. For example, the insertion of a photographic scope such as a speculum or anoscope to determine signs of vaginal or anal lacerations, bruising, abrasions, redness, swelling, or other indications of physical trauma can be both uncomfortable and scary, even if necessary, in evidence collection. In addition to a visual inspection of the genitals, photographs of the genitals and other areas of the body may be taken. Questions will be asked about any recent sexual activity prior to the attack, including any prior intimate relations with her attacker. Testing for pregnancy or the presence of drugs is common, and the victim will be treated for sexually transmitted infections. From the victim's perspective, such standard procedures may seem invasive and another form of violation. It is important that medical examiners explain each step in the procedure, especially if the victim is a minor.

Even if a victim does not want to contact the police, she nevertheless should be encouraged to receive a medical exam. She may have injuries not visible that require medical attention. In addition, if she changes her mind and reports the assault to police, such medical evidence will strengthen the case against the assailant. If she still does not want to seek medical care, at the least you can help by securing home test kits for sexually transmitted infections and pregnancy. Such test kits are available in most pharmacies at a modest cost.

As a further concern, if the rape is reported, she likely will have to recount the incident several times in detail to the police and to prosecutors, all of whom are strangers. Such questioning may take place in more than one sitting over the course of several days. Although evidence collection requires detailed interviews, this process may appear to the victim as intrusive. She may be especially reluctant to discuss certain sexually explicit elements of the rape, such as suffering anal penetration, being forced to place the perpetrator's penis in her mouth, or being graphically photographed in sexualized ways. At the very moment she needs sympathetic understanding, these standard investigative procedures can add to her fears and feelings of humiliation.

To ease her apprehensions, she may be offered the choice of having a female officer conduct the interview, though the ability to convey

Why Some Victims of Rape Remain Silent

Why might victims of rape not want to tell anyone about what happened? From an outside point of view, an unwillingness to disclose may seem unreasonable. After all, why would a victim of rape not want to seek help or the protection of law enforcement? From a victim's point of view, however, the decision to remain silent may involve a rational calculation of the risks of disclosure. The following are some of the reasons why a victim of rape may not reveal the assault:

- Desire to protect family, friends, or intimate partners from turmoil

- Distrust of the police or a belief that they cannot help

- Desire to avoid confrontation because of her choice of lifestyle or companions

- Fear others would not believe her, would blame her, or would reject her

- Fear of retaliation from the perpetrator

- For a minor, a belief that parents or guardians would restrict her independence, deny her access to friends, or impose curfews on her

- Geographical distance (e.g., being away at school) from support of family

- Social isolation (i.e., not being close enough with others to trust them with the information)

- Desire not to reveal a prior relationship with perpetrator (e.g., an ex-partner)

- Fear she will have to reveal her sexual orientation or sexual activities sympathetic understanding may be more important than the gender of the interviewer. Investigators may allow a victim advocate trained in sexual assault cases to be present during questioning. In some cases, depending on the age of the victim and the interview procedures in that jurisdiction, a family member or other support person may be present. That said, this person's presence should be at the request of

- Desire to protect perpetrator from getting into trouble and having his life "ruined"

- Victim's belief that she was at least partially responsible for the assault (self-blame)

- Victim's use of drugs or alcohol at time of assault

- Not wanting to reveal attending a social gathering connected with the assault

- Fear of gossip about what transpired, including unwanted statements on social media

- Conflicting narratives if the perpetrator operates within the same social network as the victim

- The sexually explicit details of the assault are too horrific and embarrassing to discuss

These are understandable reasons why a victim of rape may decide not to report the crime to authorities or discuss it with family members and friends. Disclosure can set in motion forces she may feel are beyond her control, and this fear of a lack of control is often coupled with a sense of her being blamed for what happened. Even if she partially discloses, she may not want to give further details, or she may minimize what happened. If she withholds some information, as a support person it is important to resist the conclusion that she is being untruthful or that her reasons for not wanting to discuss the assault are invalid. Remember, many rape victims do not share every detail of what happened for various reasons and because, in part, few recall all the details at once.

the victim. Police do not want a victim to be inhibited in her responses to questions by the presence of someone she did not ask to be there. Police also do not want someone answering questions for a victim, which sometimes happens when a parent or guardian is present. Finally, any support person present at a victim's request cannot have been a witness to what transpired.

Although most medical and legal professionals are sympathetic and try not to further distress a victim, it is possible she might encounter some who appear to her as callous or indifferent. She might feel there is implied judgment of her sexual orientation or her sexual history by those taking the report. She might feel as though they are implying she is responsible for putting herself in a position of being raped and blaming her for what happened. She might encounter those who feel she is exaggerating or misrepresenting the actions of her attacker. She may encounter insensitive remarks or even jokes about the sexual aspects of the assault. She may perceive negative judgments if her lifestyle and conduct clash with the values of others. And if the sexual assault occurred on a college campus, she may experience ineffective responses by school officials. For these and other reasons, it takes great courage for victims of sexual assault to come forward and speak about what happened. (See the inset "Why Some Victims of Rape Remain Silent" on page 30.)

RESPONDING TO HER DISCLOSURE

When a teenage or adult woman discloses that she was raped, often there is a common initial response among the men closest to her: strong anger combined with a desire to seek revenge against the rapist. Perhaps as a protective response, fathers, brothers, husbands, close male friends, and intimate male partners of victims may feel enraged and want retribution. Given that most rapes involve a perpetrator and victim who know one another, the men in a victim's life could easily gain information on her perpetrator's identity and location. Such knowledge, coupled with an impulse to "get the guy," can lead to a volatile situation that can be seriously detrimental to the victim.

In the immediate aftermath of rape, a victim needs gentleness and calmness from others when she reveals what happened. This is a time when reasoned judgment rather than angry impulses should guide decisions. As a man who cares for her, no matter how understandable your desire for retribution may be, the worst thing you could do would be to contact the alleged rapist. Threats of vengeance against the perpetrator, or any attack on his person or property, will create legal jeopardy for you and significantly add to her emotional burden. Displays of anger and threats against the rapist may likely have the opposite effect of making the victim feel safe and supported. Such threats of reprisal can add to her emotional burden by placing her in the position of now having to worry about your personal and legal safety if you should take the law into your own hands.

Threats against the perpetrator are also problematic because they shift attention from the victim's needs to yours. At a time when she most requires nurturance and understanding, your anger becomes the focus rather than her recovery. If you constantly express your anger at what happened, she may feel responsible for adding to your emotional distress. She now is in the awkward position of feeling the need to nurture you rather than the reverse. In addition, your anger can have the unintended effect of cutting off communication with her. She may feel unable to discuss the assault because it only upsets you. She may also feel guilty for "imposing" such an emotional burden on you. Understand that threats directed toward the perpetrator do not give her comfort or make her feel safe. They silence her.

Another concern for you to consider is this: Volatile expressions of anger and threats of violence from you toward the perpetrator add a measure of unpredictability to interactions with the victim. Because the stability and predictability of her everyday life has been shattered by a violent act, you should ask yourself several important questions: What happens if now you lose emotional control and vow to "get even" with the perpetrator? Will that truly make her feel safer? Will interactions with you be a "safe space" for her to process what happened? Will your behavior complicate any interactions she has with law enforcement? Because she was the target of a violent act, could your expressions of having violent intent toward the perpetrator now cause her to fear you? If you let your anger dominate the situation, most likely your lines of communication with her will be reduced and her sense of stability in her relationship with you will be diminished.

There is one final complexity regarding the consequences of displays of anger and the wish for retribution against a rapist, one that can produce significant conflicts with a victim. For many of the reasons stated earlier, she may refuse to report the crime to law enforcement. Your desire for justice and to hold the perpetrator accountable can place you at odds with the victim's wishes. Remember, rape robs a woman of her sense of control over her life. If you demand that she report the crime, or you act against her will and independently contact the police, you also rob her of the right to choose the course of action she desires.

Equally significant is the possibility that your anger toward the perpetrator may get redirected toward the victim if she does not cooperate with your demand that the crime be reported to the police. Anger directed toward a rape victim who chooses not to involve the police undermines both her recovery and her relationship with you. As a person who wants to help in her recovery, you should support her decision in this matter, even if it is contrary to your view on the matter.

There are ways, however, to respect her decision, maintain confidentiality, and provide her with support while also trying to do something positive in this situation. The Rape, Abuse & Incest National Network (RAINN) is available at the national level to guide victims of rape and their support persons. (See the Resources on page 145.) Anonymous callers, including the men in a victim's support network, receive help from professionals who can answer questions and share resources. In addition, rape crisis centers that employ counselors and victim advocates exist in most communities. They provide enormously valuable direct services to victims of sexual violence and to others. As a man who wants to help, you are encouraged to seek the guidance of these professionals. Doing so may also put you in a better position to encourage a victim to seek help. These professionals can provide counseling and other services without necessarily including the police, if such is a victim's wish.

You can contact these centers independent of the victim, given their emphasis on confidentiality, and ask for guidance. You can also ask her permission to have professional advocates contact her. These resource persons are available free of charge and work to provide victims and others with options. At the very least, your efforts to secure professional guidance will show the victim that you care and want to be a positive part of her recovery.

CONCLUSION

In the immediate aftermath of a sexual assault, there are certain core messages you should communicate to the victim upon her disclosure of what transpired. Remember, it is an act of courage and trust for a victim to share with you that she was raped. How you respond to that disclosure will set the stage for what unfolds next in her recovery and in her communications with you. There are four interrelated messages you need to communicate to her upon disclosure. They center on themes of belief, absence of blame, trust, and sustained support.

- Many rape victims remain silent out of fear that they will not be believed. You can provide a powerful message of reassurance by telling a victim you believe her, even if some may question her version of events.

- Even if a victim does not voice it, she likely is worried that she may be blamed for what happened. Let her know you do not in any way believe she was responsible for the assault. She is not to blame for the actions of the perpetrator.

- Part of the recovery process for a victim of rape is regaining control over her life. This includes her making decisions about various courses of action. Let her know you trust her ability to make good decisions for herself and do not call into question her judgment.

- Recovery from the trauma of rape is a process that unfolds over time. Express your care for her by telling her that you will stand by her no matter what. Let her know you are a steadfast ally and assure her that you will accompany her on her journey toward recovery, no matter how long it may take.

These are basic messages following her disclosure that have profound implications for what transpires next. If she knows you neither doubt her nor blame her, and that you trust her and will stand by her, it will strengthen your relationship and enhance her prospects for a full recovery. These core messages form the basis for other lines of communication that are important over the short term and long term. The next chapter discusses the things to do and not do in your communications with her.

3.

Communicating with the Victim and Others

Rape may cause many of a victim's most valued relationships to undergo a period of strain. Normal routines are disrupted and uncertainty over how to handle the complex mix of emotions often prevails. Given the turmoil she is experiencing, if there is an absence of good communication with you and others, tensions can arise. Over time, if communication erodes, mutual feelings of frustration, helplessness, and even resentment can emerge, creating even more stress on her—and on you. This chapter focuses on effective communication strategies that can strengthen your relationship and pave the way for her recovery.

BEGINNING A DIALOG

When someone decides to share a difficult experience, this person is both extending an invitation to a relationship and taking a risk. The risk resides in whether the other person will understand and accept the complexity of the speaker's experience, or whether there will be judgments, rejection, blame, misunderstanding, and loss of connection with that person. The story is an invitation to a relationship in the sense that the listener is asked to experience the world from the point of view of the person speaking, including the emotions, thoughts, and decisions of the speaker. A disclosure of rape can bring people closer together or create barriers between them, depending on the responses of the listener.

Each of the communication suggestions in this chapter flows from a common base: your ability to listen, to be empathic, and to be a supportive presence in the life of a rape victim. A positive step in her recovery from rape is her willingness and ability to talk about what happened, and this is more likely to occur if she knows she will find support from you and others. Your response to her revelation of rape will help to create fertile ground for her to grow in her own understanding of the event. Your response also helps shape the relative weight she gives this negative event as one element in the totality of her life. Your communications with her should affirm her strength, her sense of power, and the fact that she is far more than what was done to her.

When she is ready to talk to you, ask her if she wants this information to be held in confidence between the two of you, or if it may be shared with other people of her choosing. Again, communicate a core message of support. Let her know that she is not to blame for what happened. Let her know you trust that she will make good decisions in order to recover, and that you will stand by her throughout this journey of recovery. Under no circumstances should you communicate to her that you will seek revenge and "get" the perpetrator.

What You Should Not Say or Do

Beyond the basic messages of support mentioned above, there are messages you *should not* convey after a victim has shared information about her sexual assault with you.

- Listen but do not interrogate. Do not pepper her with questions and demand immediate responses to all your concerns. She may not have had sufficient time to sort out all she is feeling, and she may not wish to divulge certain details because she is deeply embarrassed. It is especially important that you refrain from unintentionally humiliating her by prying into the sexually explicit details of the rape. Victims of rape often use vague or general language in reference to the graphic sexual aspects of the assault. Allow her the freedom to discuss such details if she wishes to do so—or not to discuss them, if that is her decision.

- Never equate rape with having sex or making love, and absolutely do not imply that she may have secretly enjoyed the experience. Rape is a violent act and not a source of pleasure. Do not ask her if she experienced sexual arousal during the rape. Do not imply that she must have desired sex if there was a degree of consensual intimacy such as kissing prior to the assault. It is essential for her to know that you do not equate her victimization with an act of promiscuity or infidelity, and that you do not see her as having acted at all questionably before the assault.

- Do not be overprotective of her. Do not discourage her from engaging in normal routines of her choosing. Unless it is her decision, resist the impulse to have her accept the equivalent of twenty-four-hour surveillance. Such monitoring could unintentionally reinforce her feelings of vulnerability and powerlessness. It could also discourage her from mobilizing her own resources for coping. Your goal is not to control her path to recovery, but rather to empower her to build self-confidence. Be careful not to encourage her feelings that she has lost control over her life and is no longer self-reliant. Such overprotection might also feel so intrusive that she rebels against your attempts to be helpful.

- Never suggest that her actions may have allowed the assault to occur. This includes not shifting the focus of blame toward an adolescent victim who may have been using alcohol or drugs at the time of the rape.

- Avoid the use of patronizing language. For example, do not say you know how she feels when only she truly knows. Do not tell her "everything will be alright" when clearly that is not the case. Be careful not to trivialize or minimize the gravity of what happened by relying on trite expressions intended to soothe.

- Do not express resentment toward her or suggest she may be holding back more information because she did not tell you about the rape sooner. Such expressions will likely silence her. Expect that she may not divulge all the details of the rape right away. She may need time to sort things out, or she may be trying to protect you and others from the turmoil caused by her disclosure. A delay in disclosure or a partial disclosure should not be interpreted as rejection of you or as an effort to conceal something.

- If the legal system is involved and the victim is an adult, do not tell her what she should or should not say to the police or prosecutors.

Do not make legal decisions for her or demand that she follow a particular course of action in her dealings with law enforcement.

- If she shares information with others that she did not share with you, do not interpret this act as her rejection of or lack of trust in you. Furthermore, do not break her confidence by asking others what she may have told them. Allow her the right to find her voice with you and with others in whatever way she desires.

- Do not touch or hold her without asking permission, or unless she indicates that such comfort is welcome. Some rape victims are very sensitive about being touched or hugged following an assault, while others may welcome it as comforting. It is safest to ask first.

- Do not try to lift her spirits by making jokes or funny comments about what happened. Your role is to listen and be supportive, not to lighten the mood by making the incident seem humorous.

- Do not react surprised or negatively if her memory of what happened changes. Expect memory problems and do not become upset if her recollections are disjointed. As discussed earlier, a traumatic experience can cause a person's memory to become fragmented. Piecing together all the details of what happened may take weeks. Memory problems may also occur if the incident included the use of drugs or alcohol. Certain cues she encounters over time may trigger a memory that escaped her earlier recollection. This is normal and not an indication of deception. Do not lose your patience or trust in her as her story unfolds over time.

What You Should Say or Do

To make it easier for her to speak about the rape, be mindful of your nonverbal responses to her disclosure. Eye contact, facial expressions, nodding your head, tone of voice, and body language are all forms of communication. For example, it is important to maintain eye contact with her throughout. Fidgeting, having a downward gaze, having a lack of eye contact, seeming disinterested, texting, checking your cell phone for messages, or engaging in other distractions may make her feel as though you do not want her to talk about the incident. It is important to make her feel that you are interested in what she is saying and that she is not imposing an emotional burden on you. There are important messages of support you *should* convey to her as you listen.

- Acknowledge that it takes courage for her to risk revealing what happened. Also acknowledge that you understand how difficult it must be for her to find the right words to describe such a terrible experience. Thank her for trusting you to share this information. Let her know you are there to be supportive and listen. Your goal is to convey a calm, approachable, and nonjudgmental demeanor that encourages her to speak openly about her experience.

- Allow her to discuss what happened at a pace that is comfortable for her. When beginning a conversation, it is appropriate to ask "what" and "how" questions carefully at the right moments. Examples may include the following:

  o What happened next? How did that make you feel?

  o What do you most fear?

  o What would you like to see happen now?

  o How can I be of most help to you at this moment?

  Equally important is to avoid asking questions that begin with the word "why." Examples may include the following:

  o Why were you at that place at that time?

  o Why didn't you scream and run?

  o Why did you talk to him in the first place?

  o Why were you drinking or using drugs?

  o Why were you so friendly to him?

  o Why were you alone with him?

  Not only do such "why" questions unintentionally imply negative judgments, but they also may make her feel guilty or even resentful toward you. They also are likely to make her less willing to talk to you or others about what happened.

- Reassure her that she did not cause someone to rape her. Focus on the fact that she was the target of a crime. It is the rapist alone who is responsible for the attack. Let her know that you do not accept the myth that a victim triggers a violent and uncontrollable impulse in a perpetrator and therefore is to blame for his actions. This myth is one of the most injurious forms of victim blaming, and a key reason why so many victims of sexual violence are reluctant to disclose what happened. (See the inset "The Enduring Myth of Victim-Precipitated Rape" on page 44.)

- Make sure she knows she is not responsible for failing to resist the attack or for "not fighting hard enough" to ward off the assault. Remind her that rapists use physical and psychological forces to over-power women, and that many victims are paralyzed by fear during an attack. Failure to resist, including not physically fighting back when overpowered, is *never* to be interpreted as implied consent. Reaffirm the fact that what matters is that she survived the assault. When she is ready, encourage her to discuss with a counselor any misconceptions about rape, which may be contributing to her emotional state. Again, reassure her that you do not accept unfounded ideas that place blame on a victim or suggest that her actions encouraged the behavior of a perpetrator. The blame is entirely on the perpetrator, not her.

- Acknowledge that fear and general feelings of anxiety or apprehen-sion are normal reactions among rape victims following an assault. Remember that the perpetrator may have threatened retaliation against her (or others) to prevent her from revealing what happened. Let her know you do not believe her fears and anxieties are an overreaction to what happened but an understandable response to an extreme event. This includes frightening flashbacks, which she may experience. Acknowledging her justifiable apprehension creates a safe space for her to talk about that which is preoccupying her thoughts. Although more will be said about this in the next chapter, talking about one's fears, including flashbacks, is a positive step toward healing.

- When asked, acknowledge what probably is obvious to her: the fact that the rape has triggered in her an array of difficult emotions such as anger, sadness, confusion, apprehension, guilt, and uncertainty. It is important to be emotionally honest about how the rape has shaken both of you. Telling her that the assault has not affected her or you would likely appear to her as untruthful.

- Pay special attention to any aspects of the assault that she frequently mentions as she talks about what happened and how they have affected her. Recurrent conversational topics might provide insight into the things that most bother her. Be aware that one outcome of rape is that it can bring to the surface unfinished business in a victim's life, including problems that existed before the assault. This may include any number of troubling things, such as prior or current difficult relationships, family or personal substance abuse, bullying, or the death of a family member or friend. If there were prior experiences of physical or sexual victimization at another time in her life, those negative experiences may again surface and become linked emotionally and psychologically to this latest incident.

- If experiences of prior victimization emerge and seem unresolved for her, do not act shocked or dismayed. Instead acknowledge that it is common for other terrible experiences to reemerge in one's mind when confronted with another trauma. Try to stay focused on the current situation unless it is her wish to elaborate on those earlier events. Given the complex interplay of her prior and current traumatic experiences, however, you should strongly encourage her to speak with a professional counselor.

COMMUNICATING WITH OTHERS

When someone is sexually assaulted, close friends and family members often respond in the same ways as the victim, which frequently include shock, denial, anger, confusion, and feelings of injustice. These reactions reflect attempts to make sense of an event that is cruel and unjust. As others consider what happened, however, there is a tendency for some to make comments that may be insensitive, unhelpful, or reflective of their misconceptions about rape. This can have the effect of increasing rather than reducing the rape victim's emotional burden. You can help by serving as a buffer between her and others who may not fully understand her circumstances. There are several ways to do this without alienating those in contact with the victim.

The Enduring Myth of Victim-Precipitated Rape

Among the most enduring and troubling misunderstandings about sexual violence is the idea that victims willingly participate in a chain of events that triggers a response in perpetrators and results in rape. This myth is called *victim-precipitated rape*. The assumption is that if women are drinking alcohol and attending social gatherings unaccompanied, they are seen by men as engaging in provocative acts that invite and justify the actions of a perpetrator. In essence, this myth suggests that women who are "reckless" in their dress or behavior knowingly give off cues that precipitate the actions of rapists.

This false argument reflects, reinforces, and gives the veneer of legitimacy to perhaps the most harmful and enduring myth about rape: the view that women are to blame for the actions of their rapists. Women *do not* cause uncontrollable and violent sexual assaults perpetrated by men. This form of blaming the victim, though widely criticized, persists to this day and has had truly unfortunate consequences. For example, defense attorneys in rape cases have seized upon the dubious notion of victim-precipitated rape to reduce charges or avoid penalties for their clients. The victim's reputation and behavior are often placed on trial in court as if she is the true instigator of the perpetrator's criminal acts. It is anyone's guess how much this undo scrutiny discourages victims from reporting the crime or pursuing criminal action against their assailants.

Shifting blame to the victim also seems to justify the actions of a perpetrator, who can claim that she "lead him on" or was being a "tease." By invoking this view, it is as if the perpetrator is suggesting that his "sexual rights" were somehow violated and she therefore got what she had coming. It is important to understand that the underlying motivation for rape is male contempt for women combined with a desire to control and humiliate them. It is not motivated by an uncontrollable sexual impulse in men prompted by their victims. This persistent myth is among the chief reasons why victims often suffer in silence, as they fear being blamed if they speak out. A victim of sexual assault is not responsible for the actions of a rapist; the rapist is.

- Discourage family and friends from contacting or threatening revenge against the attacker. Such threats arise partly out of a sincere desire to affirm their support for the victim and partly to counteract their own feelings of helplessness. As previously discussed, such threats do little to reassure rape victims and can cause further trauma. These threats could also complicate any dealings she may have with law enforcement.

- Others can unintentionally place an additional burden on the victim when they continually express their own feelings of anger, frustration, or helplessness. Such constant expressions of intense emotions can heighten her anxieties and seem overwhelming to her and should therefore be discouraged.

- Given how often rape victims and perpetrators know one another, there is a high probability that a victim and her attacker share the same social circle. Quite simply, a victim's friends may also be friends with the person who raped her. Whatever their private views of this person, any comments that "he is not that kind of guy," or of "not wanting to take sides," should not be communicated to her. If her friends make such comments to you, respond by indicating it is not about "taking sides," but rather about a violent act and her need to recover. Be very clear about two things: You do not want anyone to share with her their views about the character of the person who assaulted her, and you do not want them to share information with the perpetrator about "how she is doing."

- Dissuade others from making insensitive jokes about rape. Advise them that sexualized humor is likely to increase the victim's confusion and isolation, and perhaps cause her to distrust those who truly want to be helpful. Inappropriate humor may also reinforce her fears about how she thinks others perceive her. That said, there are times when watching a funny movie with friends, laughing together about silly things, or other lighthearted communication can be a good way to raise spirits, if it is something she wishes.

- Let the victim decide when a diversion such as going to a movie or attending a social gathering would be appropriate. She will not recover sooner from an attack simply because others tell her not to think about it or do things to take her mind off it. It is counterproductive to engage in a "friendly conspiracy" with others to distract the victim by acting as if the rape never happened. She could interpret these diversions to mean that her family and friends regard the assault as too awful to discuss, or too trivial to acknowledge. True, there are appropriate times when she might want to engage in diversions, but this should be at her request.

- Respect the victim's wishes for confidentiality and encourage others to do the same. She should decide what information to disclose and with whom it should be discussed. Remember, in the aftermath of rape, victims are often reluctant to discuss the attack. Others, however, may interpret such reluctance to talk as an unhealthy withdrawal. In addition, in a well-intended effort to be helpful, others might solicit assistance from friends, clergy, or mental-health professionals. Such attempts to intervene, unless requested by the victim, should be discouraged.

- Help safeguard her need for privacy. Sometimes it is desirable and therapeutic for her to process her feelings alone. A constant stream of well-wishers, especially in the immediate aftermath of the assault, can be an emotional drain. She may ask you to let others know on her behalf of her desire for privacy. In respecting the victim's wish for privacy, you will reinforce the view that she is the best judge of what she needs.

- Remind family and friends that they should never imply the attack was caused by what the victim did or did not do. Such second-guessing is a form of victim blaming that reinforces guilt and self-blame.

- Let others know that rape trauma can cause confusion and memory problems in victims. Even if not all the details of the assault appear consistent or coherent, others should not express doubts about the fundamental truth of the victim's account of what transpired.

- Discourage others from asking the victim questions about the nature and content of any counseling or medical attention she may be receiving. This is private information that requires her sole discretion to discuss.

- Remind others not to post information on social media about the rape or the status of her recovery. A cascade of gossip and misinformed speculation would be counterproductive to the victim's wellbeing. If unfortunate comments are posted on social media and you learn about them, it would be appropriate, with the victim's permission, to politely ask the person who posted the comments to remove them.

Because the circle of family and immediate friends of a rape victim can help add stability to her life, it is important to keep all these points in mind. There is, however, an added element of complexity that requires great care in navigating: social media. The time we now live in has opened a new dimension of communication, one that can take on a life of its own with little control. It is therefore important to be aware of how the world of social media can intersect with the life of a rape victim and with those who care about her.

SOCIAL MEDIA

We live in a society of instant electronic communication. The world of social media is central to how many people access information and share their views. On the internet, information travels at an extraordinarily fast rate, with all the accompanying distortions, judgments, and interpretations. It is almost impossible for a subject of online discourse to control the nature and flow of personal information.

Regardless of age or social circumstance, a person victimized by sexual violence may become the object of gossip-filled narratives on social media. Often those who are sharing information know the victim. This includes friends, family, peers at school, and casual acquaintances. Such commenters generally fall into one of several types. First, there are those who want to demonstrate support for the rape victim and then use social media platforms to express their outrage. Second, there are people who perhaps use more neutral language and simply share the "news," including detailed information about the assault (e.g., "Did you hear what happened to …?"). Finally, there are those who express an opinion or judgment about the victim's behavior and the circumstances surrounding the assault. Information and judgments also might be shared about the alleged perpetrator.

The problems such communications pose for victims of rape are significant. Typically, these social media posts are shared without a victim's consent. What a person believes is private and confidential can quickly become public, with little anyone can do to stop the flow of speculation—and often misinformation—which can take on a momentum of its own. Those who post this information, even if they intend no harm, generally fail to ask themselves, "What will this do to the person?" Furthermore, if the sexual assault is under police scrutiny, social media speculation can complicate investigative efforts and may introduce bias into court proceedings. It also gives the perpetrator a chance to see "what's out there" and perhaps concoct a cover story.

When Victims Use Social Media

Does use of the internet, especially access to social media, pose a special risk to victims of rape? The simple answer is there is no simple answer. It is true that any rape victim might find disturbing online content that could trigger an upsetting response. This may include anything from graphic violence to the comments of others. On the flip side, it is also true that there are resources and support groups for rape victims online. Equally important, a victim's ability to communicate with friends on social media can also be beneficial.

For young people in particular, access to social media is a basic element of everyday life. It is therefore not helpful for well-meaning parents or others to try to restrict a victim's access to social media. Restricting access could even be seen by her as punishment for what happened. It is not possible or even desirable to attempt to protect victims of rape from the flow of content on social media sites. It can be helpful, however, to ask a victim how she feels or what she might do if she encounters something online that upsets her. It is a better option to encourage her to talk with you or a counselor about what she may find on the web, rather than trying to protect her from every possible source of information that might be hurtful.

Sexual violence denies victims a right to choose. Social media speculation about victims is a further denial of their rights. In the wake of an assault, it is important to remind all who know of the event to refrain from using social media to express outrage, share news, or otherwise offer opinions about what transpired. If news of the sexual assault already is a widely shared topic on social media, with the victim's permission there is the option of posting a brief statement acknowledging people's concerns but asking them to refrain from further comment. Responding individually to every single post on social media is to be discouraged, however, as it is likely to boost further comment and speculation.

As someone who cares about her recovery, use your contacts with others to establish an accepting, nonjudgmental climate in which she can express painful feelings without fear of criticism. If she finds something about the assault on social media, discuss with her how she thinks others may be interpreting the event. She needs to know that you believe her family and friends do not hold her responsible for what happened, and that she is not diminished as a woman because she was attacked. What truly matters is that she survived.

TRAUMA AND CONFUSION

There is a final concern about communication with her that was hinted at earlier in this book and is worth considering further. Although it is difficult to admit, even the most loving and caring man may have unanswered questions or doubts about what he has been told by a rape victim. He may privately question whether some things are intentionally omitted from her story. He may question why some aspects of her description about the rape have changed over time. He might wonder why she took so long to reveal what happened. And he may be unsettled by what appear to be inconsistencies and gaps in her account of the rape. As a result of such lingering doubts, a subtle implied judgment about her credibility may be conveyed, one that could silence her and hinder the relationship.

Even if her account appears incomplete or confused, do not automatically conclude that she has misrepresented what happened or was being deliberately untruthful. Most rape victims do not recall or necessarily share every detail of what happened. As previously discussed, memory problems connected to trauma, embarrassment, shame, fear of judgment, and other factors may shape how she speaks about what was done to her. Remember that survivors of trauma generally recall bits and pieces of what happened over time, and each recounting of the event is therefore likely to change to some degree.

It is rather like looking into shards of a shattered mirror and trying to produce a coherent image for oneself and for others. Some details will be emphasized over others, some will be modified with better recollection, and some will be omitted altogether. For example, teenage victims of rape who are not of legal drinking age often minimize the extent of their alcohol consumption because they fear punishment. The important point to understand is that a degree of confusion or omission is normal in the narrative accounts of rape victims.

Remember this: Very few women make false claims about being raped. It is not helpful for you to question the reality of her victimization because some elements of her account do not meet your expectations. By its very nature, trauma causes confusion. One way to quell doubts you may have is to speak with a rape crisis counselor who can explain the complex reasons why victims of rape tell their stories in a particular fashion. Perhaps the most important thing you can do is also the simplest: Tell her that even if you do not understand all the details of what happened, you do not doubt the truth of what she has told you. If she knows you believe her, this will help in her recovery and strengthen the foundation of your relationship.

CONCLUSION

The communications you have directly with a rape survivor and with others in her social network can shape the character and timing of her recovery. The core messages of believing her, not blaming her, trusting her, and standing by her are what both you and others need to share with her. Her ability to talk about what happened and find support in this process becomes the foundation upon which she can reclaim power over her life. Your task is to help create an accepting climate in which she can move forward on this journey. Trust that she has the strength and determination to do the rest on her own.

4.

Understanding the Long-Term Effects of Rape

What are the consequences of rape for survivors over a long period of time? While this is a straightforward question, it does have not a simple answer. There are both predictable features in the recovery process and substantial variations in how different people are affected by sexual violence. On one hand, the process of recovery from rape is highly individualized and can depend on any combination of factors. These factors include the age of victim, the relationship of the victim to the perpetrator, any previous experiences of trauma, the victim's mental state prior to the assault and after, the degree of physical injury caused by the assault, the nature and extent of violence experienced during the attack, and the type of support system available to the victim following the rape. The speed of her recovery will be influenced by many of these elements.

On the other hand, despite individual differences, psychologists have found that the recovery process for many survivors reflects a common pattern, which is measured in stages. For some, progression through these stages is relatively quick; for others, it may take years. This chapter focuses on these stages, describes how the recovery process unfolds, and offers ways to enhance this process through the rape survivor's support system.

Even though the time immediately after a rape may seem chaotic and confused, family and friends who know what happened will usually show their support and try to be of assistance. Over time, however, this initial outpouring of support tends to fade away. Clearly, the consequences of rape can linger long after the immediate event and influence the thoughts and feelings of a victim for many months. The emotional ground upon which she stands may shift at unexpected moments and throw her off balance. The residual effects of sexual violence can affect not only her but also her closest relationships.

As a man who wants to help, the greatest test of your relationship may not occur immediately after a rape, but most likely in the months that follow. Although there are variations in how people recover, it is helpful to understand the common emotional responses that may be present during a victim's recovery.

COMMON EMOTIONAL RESPONSES

Even though no two victims of rape necessarily exhibit the same sequence of emotions or behaviors over time, there are common aspects to the recovery experience. For weeks or perhaps months after the assault, victims of rape may appear to be "stuck" in an emotional space where listlessness, grief, melancholy, withdrawal from others, and the absence of joyfulness seem to characterize their actions. For some, it may appear as if they are emotionally numb and not easily consoled. They may appear to "go through the motions" of everyday living but do so in a way that is seemingly detached from others.

Typically, those closest to the victim are stressed by trying to act appropriately given her emotional state of mind. In a sense, some of her stress now is taken on and shared by those who love her most. If stress is the result of encountering adversity in striving to achieve important goals in one's life, then the goal of returning to normalcy and finding happiness again may seem blocked. This can lead those around her to feel frustration at their powerlessness to alter the emotional space in which she seems stuck. Those closest to her may silently begin to ask themselves questions that reflect their frustration, such as:

- Why can't she put this behind her and move forward?

- How much longer is this going to take?

- After all the support she has been given, why can't she get back to normal?

The consequence of such questions, though unintended, may be that others gradually direct their judgment toward what seems like the source of their frustration: the rape victim. Perhaps without even knowing they are doing it, others (including you) may risk imposing their terms of recovery on her. Men close to her who feel the need to take charge may be especially prone to render judgment on the pace of her recovery. It is as if they have an internal clock indicating that now is the time for her to be better. And if she fails to conform to this unstated and arbitrary timetable for recovery, she is somehow responsible for not fighting hard enough to get over it. It is at this point that one's relationship with the victim undergoes the greatest strain, possibly to the point of causing irreparable damage.

There is an important reason why you and others may feel frustrated at what appears to be the slow course of her recovery. Even though she may be progressing at a solid pace, as one who cares for her you may think the opposite is happening—that she is moving in the wrong direction. Quite simply, you may not understand the long-term effects of sexual trauma and the normal stages of recovery common among victims. In the absence of such understanding, the tendency is to have unrealistic expectations of her recovery.

Self-Interrogation and Pre-Impact Terror

In the weeks or months following a rape, the victim often engages in a process known as *self-interrogation*—in other words, evaluating one's own conduct. She may ask herself questions such as:

- Why did this happen to me?

- Why did I let this happen?

- Why didn't I behave differently?

- What did I do to cause him to attack me?

- How could I have been so foolish as to trust him?

- Why do I keep thinking about this and not just let it go?

The churning of such questions can be debilitating, especially if others unintentionally reinforce the view that these questions have merit. One source of this self-interrogation has its origins in what happened immediately before the rape. Victims of sexual assault commonly experience *pre-impact terror*. This term refers to the frightening moments just prior to the attack when the victim may know what is about to happen yet is powerless to stop it. The basis of pre-impact terror is the realization that one will be intentionally harmed and there is no escape, and the fear that one's life may never be the same again. Then, as the impact of the attack unfolds, many victims report experiencing an intense wave of simultaneously conflicting emotions: denial, disbelief, extreme fear, injustice, disorientation, and possibly a feeling of leaving one's body.

Victims often relive these moments and blame themselves for failing to prevent what occurred. They may also impose on themselves an unreasonable standard of conduct based upon how they feel they should or should not have responded to the attack. It is as if they say

Male Anger

The emotional pain and sadness a rape victim feels has a ripple effect that often touches the men in her life. Males, too, experience a range of emotional shifts, which may include shock, uncertainty, sadness, and anxiety. Some men also experience feelings of guilt or self-blame for what they perceive as a failure to protect a loved one. In a sense, a challenge to her recovery is the challenge of the men in her life struggling to deal with their own complex emotions following the rape.

One emotion especially can surface in many men and complicate a victim's recovery while also negatively affecting her relationship with these men. It should be no surprise that many men experience intense anger when a child, adolescent, or adult woman they love has been raped. This anger might be described as impotent rage—a desire to strike back at the rapist but having no means to do so. An expression of this anger is a common experience of revenge fantasies about getting even with a rapist. These thoughts reflect an understandable yearning for retribution, especially if legal means of doing so are not available. Of course, acting on such fantasies is both inappropriate and legally problematic. Although it is not a good idea to share such revenge to themselves, "What if I had done this?" or "I should have done that." Even though they were in a situation that permitted no choice, some victims beat themselves down with this relentless processing of "what ifs." They seem to forget that at the time, they faced a threat to their lives or were incapacitated and unable to act. Such second-guessing is a form of self-blame.

Should this be the case, a helpful thing you can do is to discuss what she is feeling and simply acknowledge that second-guessing herself in the wake of a traumatic experience is common and understandable. She needs assurance that it was not her fault and that she acted reasonably under the circumstances, and she needs a reminder that she was given no choice. Again, the message from you should be consistent: She is not to blame, and she did not cause this to happen. It is important for

fantasies with a victim, it is helpful to talk about these thoughts with a professional counselor.

There is another danger posed by such feelings of anger. The intense anger directed toward the rapist can sometimes unintention- ally be redirected toward the victim. Such anger may be expressed as bitter resentment at how lives have been upended by the rape and the challenges of her recovery. This transference is a gradual and subtle process of which men may not be aware. How might this happen? Over time, initial support for a rape victim may fade and be replaced by resentment at her needs. Ironically, men often encour- age rape victims to rely on them and then gradually resent what may seem like dependence. In addition, as a rape victim struggles through the ups and downs of the recovery process, some men may think she is using her victimization as an excuse to avoid certain respon- sibilities. They grow to resent what they perhaps mistakenly believe is manipulation, or they resent that her recovery is taking too long.

Obviously, the turmoil caused by rape weighs heavily on the patience and resources of all concerned. As a guard against feeling anger and resentment toward a rape victim, men need to remind themselves to be patient and trust in her ability to recover. Allowing their anger to shift toward the victim of rape is destructive and benefits no one.

both of you to remember that these reactions are normal responses to a terrifying, life-threatening experience.

You should also acknowledge that you are not second-guessing her actions or imposing on her any standard regarding ways in which she might have acted differently. Furthermore, when necessary, let her know that you think she is being too hard on herself in regard to what she may feel she could have done differently. It is important to remember that rape involves the opportunistic imposition of power over a target who is vulnerable. Remind her that she was not in control of the perpetrator's actions. Feeling guilt or second-guessing will never alter this fact. Again, because she survived, she did the right thing.

RAPE TRAUMA SYNDROME

Therapists have identified a separate type of post-traumatic stress disorder specific to rape victims called *rape trauma syndrome*, or *RTS* (also referred to as *rape-related post-traumatic stress disorder*). Although various symptoms of RTS overlap with PTSD, a person may exhibit signs of RTS without necessarily having all the full-blown clinical symptoms of PTSD. PTSD reflects many kinds of traumatic experiences, not just sexual assault. Rape trauma syndrome is specific to persons who have been the target of rape, attempted rape, or other forms of abusive sexual contact, regardless of whether the perpetrator is a friend, family member, acquaintance, or stranger.

Rape trauma syndrome describes the progression that may unfold from the initial shock immediately after the rape to the coming to terms with that experience over a long period of time. Experts in the field of sexual trauma generally agree on three stages of RTS, though it may be best to think of them as connected phases rather than separate stages.

Acute Stage

This stage typically occurs soon after the sexual assault and may last for a few days or up to several weeks. As described earlier, the victim may appear shocked, disoriented, extremely anxious, highly emotional, fearful, unable to make decisions, and possibly in a state of denial. Flashbacks, being on constant high alert, and social withdrawal are common. Given the varied nature of trauma responses, the victim may also exhibit what seems like the opposite behavior—appearing controlled and acting as if nothing significant happened. This appearance of calm, including her indications that she is fine, is a mask that may hide more unsettling emotions that are likely to surface over time.

Other indicators of emotional distress may also emerge during this acute phase, including fear, anger, grief, and a sense of shame and self-blame. Abrupt changes in mood are common. Some victims of rape at this stage may feel they are overreacting to normal everyday problems, which increases their distress. They are on an emotional roller coaster and perhaps fluctuate between extremes—at times angry, at times very withdrawn, at times near tears. Eventually, however, these intense reactions seem to subside as a new phase emerges.

Outward Adjustment Stage

As signs of acute distress diminish in the weeks and months that follow a rape, the victim often presents an outward appearance of moving forward and having put "it" behind her. She may announce that she no longer is troubled by what happened and deny that the attack continues to bother her. For those closest to her, it may seem as though things are back to normal, and the sexual assault has faded into the background. Yet the appearance of normalcy may be just that—an appearance that belies the inner turmoil she is experiencing. Even if she indicates that the assault is no longer a concern, and despite her possible refusal to even talk about it anymore, most likely the rape lingers in the background of her thoughts and affects her behavior.

Behind this appearance of normalcy, a denial that the assault still troubles her does not mean she is deliberately being deceptive. Rather, it is highly likely she feels responsible for the turmoil that has been added to the lives of those who care for her. She may feel a sense of guilt for "imposing" her emotional needs on you and others in the aftermath of the assault. Her desire not to "burden" others is a subtle force pushing her to create the appearance that she is doing fine. In addition, because she wants to believe she is progressing in her recovery, she may simply be acting as though all is well as proof to herself that things are back to normal. This is like her saying to herself, "If I simply act this way it will prove I am better." Consequently, by minimizing the seriousness of how much she remains affected by the assault, she is signaling to others and herself that she has moved on.

Notwithstanding, with this outward appearance of adjustment, there are often troubling signs that indicate the assault has not faded into the background of her life. Sleep disturbances, mood swings, flashbacks, anxiety, and other indicators of traumatic distress may abruptly reemerge. Even if she tries to hide these symptoms from others, those close to her usually notice that all is not well.

At this point, given the persistence of these symptoms, she may employ positive coping mechanisms toward greater self-care. This may include regular exercise, restoration of bodily rhythms through sleep and diet, or more reliance on the support of family or a counselor. But there is also the danger that she will be so upset at her seeming relapse that she self-medicates with alcohol or drugs. She may also attempt to cope by engaging in other high-risk behaviors, including problematic sexual behaviors. Now, after months, those closest to her may conclude, "She was getting better and now she is getting worse." It is at this very point that her relationships with those who care most for her are likely to become strained.

Although this time can be confusing and difficult for all, there is a silver lining. To the extent that trauma impairs a victim, what may be happening is that she is actively seeking ways to regain control over her life. At this phase of her recovery, it is as if she has given herself permission to reorganize her life, even if it seems to be in fits and starts. Because she now has gained a degree of distance from the assault, she is thinking through its place in her life, including who she is and who she wants to be. Such emotional processing is an important step toward healing.

Two things are especially noteworthy at this point. First, the symptoms of trauma she is experiencing are likely to be less intense than those of acute phase of recovery. Rather than experiencing symptoms in a raw and unfiltered manner as before, she is now processing what is happening with greater self-awareness. Second, if at this time she is not already seeing a therapist, she may now be willing to seek counseling. If she already is seeing a counselor, she may benefit even more from ongoing therapy sessions. In essence, she is moving toward what therapists call *integration*, or the third stage of recovery: resolution.

Resolution Stage

The process of healing and getting to this stage of recovery will be helped or hindered by the type of the support system available to her. With support from you and others, the sexual assault is no longer a central element in her life. Resolution is about her feeling empowered to control her life again, and it is about reestablishing healthy connections to others. She accepts the fact that this terrible experience happened and chooses to move forward. She may still have conflicting thoughts and emotions about the assault and its aftermath, but she now gives herself permission to hold those thoughts and feelings in a way that does not hinder her. Although what happened will not be forgotten, the rape is assimilated into the larger frame of her life and diminishes in importance. In this sense, resolution truly means that one moves from being a victim to a survivor.

One indication of having moved toward resolution is a shift in the way a survivor thinks and talks about what happened. She has gained insight and perspective not only about the assault but also herself. Self-interrogation or second-guessing about what she might have done differently, expressions of self-blame or guilt, withdrawal, and other indications of trauma experienced earlier now fade. In general, there seems to be a return to a level of emotional stability that existed prior to the assault. Even if there are occasional flashbacks, they tend to diminish in frequency and intensity.

Resolution does not necessarily mean that all aspects of her life will go back to exactly the way they were before the assault. Rather, resolution is about finding and embracing a "new normal," which often includes newly acquired strength and self-confidence. In fact, researchers in the field of trauma and recovery have identified a very positive outcome for many survivors called post-traumatic growth, or PTG. The basic idea of PTG is a hopeful one. It points out that the hardships induced by sexual trauma can, under the right conditions, become a growth experience for the survivor and those close to her. This idea is so important that Chapter 10 (see page 133) includes a full discussion of it.

Again, it's important to point out that the recovery process is not identical for all victims of rape, even though some patterns can be anticipated. Victims vary in their resilience, and in the frequency, intensity, and duration of symptoms associated with traumatic distress. Admittedly, it is a very confusing thing to make sense of the ebbs and flows inherent to responses to trauma. Just keep in mind that the process of recovery is gradual and should not be rushed. Trust that your patience and support will help a rape victim to move forward.

Despite the differences in how people recover from rape, there is a common denominator among survivors. Nearly all undergo a period of grieving after the assault. Grief is linked to trauma, and it forms the background against which the recovery process unfolds. It is therefore important to understand the nature of grief and how people cope with it as an element of rape recovery.

RAPE GRIEF

Grief is an intense emotional response to a significant personal loss. Psychologists generally describe grief as an anguished experience that includes yearning for what was lost, perhaps remorse for what one did or did not do, and apprehensions about the future. Because nearly everyone experiences grief at some point in life, it should not be thought of as a clinical condition, but rather as a natural response to loss—one that poses both challenges and opportunities for healing. Grief is only harmful when it disrupts a person's ability to function daily, causes self-neglect, and results in thoughts of self-harm. It is also powerful enough to compromises one's immune system.

Although we often attribute grief to the death of a loved one, there can be many other sources of it, including grief connected to sexual trauma, or what might be called *rape grief*. The initial shock following a rape gradually gives way to a lingering sense of loss among victims, the elements of which are rooted in what has been taken away. Consider the following kinds of loss a victim of rape may grieve following the assault:

- Loss of a sense of safety

- Loss of a feeling of mental and physical wellbeing

- Loss of trust in others

- Loss of lifestyle

- Loss of hopes and dreams about the future

- Loss of the ability to resume normal roles (such as going to school or work)

- Loss of power over one's life

- Loss of virginity (if the rape was a person's first "sexual" encounter)

- Loss of interest in physical intimacy

- Loss of significant relationships, especially if the perpetrator belongs to the victim's family or network of friends

- Loss of a sense that the world can be a kind and just place

- Loss of self-esteem

The combination and cumulation of such losses produced by rape can generate a deep sadness in rape victims. This sadness is not the same as chronic depression, though it may temporarily appear to mimic some aspects of depression. Fundamentally, chronic depression involves a generalized and protracted lack of interest in life. It may also include feelings of self-loathing to the point of despair. Grief, however, is about trying to regain or compensate for what was lost. It typically does not include feelings of self-loathing, and it generally involves a desire to regain or restore one's engagement in daily life.

The processing of rape grief is not necessarily straightforward. Like the tides, it ebbs and flows and is subject to triggers that remind a rape victim of what has been taken away. Also contained within rape grief are conflicting sentiments such as wanting to be alone yet missing time with friends, wanting to share one's concerns yet not wanting to burden others, and feeling fatigue yet being restless. And like other dimensions of trauma, a grieving person often has difficulty expressing what she is feeling at any given moment.

Dealing with Rape Grief Incorrectly

Unfortunately, much of the well-intentioned advice on how rape victims should process their trauma-related grief reflects myth and folk wisdom. Bad advice on how to cope with rape grief is worrisome because it may create self-doubts in victims that undermine the grieving process. Perhaps the most common misunderstanding about grief is contained in the expression "time heals all wounds." Although it is true that it takes

time to process grief, it is the degree of support and acceptance rape victims receive over the long run that shapes their healing. There is nothing
magical about time alone that will somehow heal deep feelings of loss.
Simply telling a rape victim to "give it time" may trivialize the gravity
of what she is experiencing and does not resolve the emotional turmoil
associated with loss. Furthermore, by telling a rape victim that only time
will heal feelings of grief, you may be unintentionally reinforcing her
feelings of powerlessness. This conveys the message that nothing she or
anyone else does will relieve her feelings of loss, that she is ultimately
alone in her suffering, and that waiting rather that deliberate action is
the only way to cope.

One misinformed piece of advice for a rape victim struggling with
loss is to suggest that she "shouldn't think about it" or "shouldn't feel
that way." Such advice is misdirected for several reasons. Telling her not
to dwell on the rape and her sense of loss equates to telling her to bury
or ignore powerful feelings. Suppressing or ignoring feelings does not
produce resolution, nor does it create an emotional space where she can
easily get on with her life. Furthermore, telling a grieving rape survivor
not to feel a certain way denies her the right to her true feelings. Finally,
such a message implies she is somehow inadequate for not rationally
controlling her emotional state.

Another piece of misguided folk wisdom about how to deal with
rape grief is to tell her to "keep busy." Immersion in work or other activities will not inevitably cause her to "snap out of it." Although there
can be therapeutic value in maintaining a work or school schedule if
accompanied by a proper support system, simply keeping busy does not
eliminate troublesome thoughts and feelings. Temporary distractions are
just that—temporary—and do not provide permanent relief from grief.

One final piece of misguided folk wisdom is to suggest that feelings
of loss can be resolved by acquiring something new. The obvious problem is that grief caused by rape is not offset by new possessions. Offers
of material objects, however well-intentioned, may be interpreted by her
as a crass attempt to buy off her sense of grief, and that having a new
object means that now she should get back to normal.

Misinformed guidance about how a rape victim should deal with
her grief can result in several unfortunate outcomes. First, she may
experience guilt for feeling or not feeling a certain way. Second, she may
become guarded in expressing to others how she truly feels for fear of

being judged or rejected. Finally, suggesting that a rape victim should bury or ignore her feelings may function to confuse her about what she is actually feeling. Remember, recovery is a process based upon honest expressions of feelings within a supportive environment. Her ability to process grief is enhanced when she is free to be honest with herself and in touch with her true feelings. Denial, guilt, and an inability to share her feelings with others is a recipe for prolonging her sense of loss.

Consider how misguided information regarding how a rape victim should deal with rape grief contributes to the possibility that she may act as if she is fully recovered even though she is still grieving. As suggested earlier, the problem of acting recovered can happen because she does not want to burden others with her sadness, nor does she want to feel isolated because others do not know how to respond to her grief. She may also imply that the well-intentioned but problematic suggestions given to her on how to cope are helping, while in actuality they are not. She now is in the awkward position of making others feel better for trying to make her feel better, though her grieving persists. As a result, both she and those who care for her may come to an unspoken understanding that it is easier to "put on a happy face" than to openly confront more complicated emotions.

The Date of the Assault

One of the enduring consequences of rape is that most victims remember the date on which the assault occurred. For survivors, the date the rape took place can trigger memories of the experience. As the date approaches, a victim's feelings of grief and other emotional complexities may surface. This is normal and not an indication of relapse. As one who cares for her wellbeing, a gesture acknowledging the relevance of this date is appropriate if she shows indications of what is on her mind. It should not surprise you if she says something about "that day," even if she has not mentioned the assault for some time. Comforting words or expressions that let her know you understand her feelings and care would be fitting. This can also be an opportunity for both of you to reflect on just how far she has progressed since that terrible event.

Dealing with Rape Grief Correctly

Among experts in the therapeutic community, there is one thing about grief resolution upon which nearly all agree: It is important for grieving persons to have a safe space to express their feelings of loss, and for others to acknowledge these feelings of loss. Finding one's voice to express grief is critical for moving through it. Writing about loss, reading stories about losses others have endured, and talking about one's grief within the context of a support group are examples of healthy ways to process grief. Such actions help a person to step away gradually from the strong emotions caused by what was lost and shift focus to the practical aspects of living her life again.

CONCLUSION

As you have read in this chapter, rape recovery is a process that unfolds gradually and is shaped by the interactions a rape survivor has with others. Although there are common patterns in the recovery process, no two survivors necessarily make sense of what happened in the same way. In general, however, the process is characterized by grief over the loss of what once was and an endeavor to see positive changes emerge from this terrible experience.

As an ally in the recovery of someone you love, your patience and unconditional support are essential. With your sustained support, she will move forward on a journey toward positive change. By giving her space to process what happened on her terms without pressuring her to "get better" on your terms, you can contribute to a more hopeful future for her.

5.

The Impact of Rape on Sexual Intimacy

For a woman who is in an intimate relationship at the time of her rape, a change in sexual behavior with her partner is common. This generally is true for both heterosexual and nonheterosexual women. Usually, this change includes a decline in sexual desire and sexual satisfaction. For adolescent and young adult women who are not in an intimate relationship at the time of a rape, anxiety about entering a romantic and potentially intimate relationship often occurs. Men who are or who might become intimate sexual partners with a rape survivor may feel confusion, apprehension, and tension about sexual intimacy. Quite simply, distress about sexual intimacy in the aftermath of a rape seems to be a common reaction in both rape victims and their partners.

While it is true that not all rape survivors experience problematic sexual outcomes, many do. There can be many factors that affect a rape victim's thoughts, emotions, and behaviors regarding sexual responsiveness. Rape seems to create a turning point for what follows in the sexual life of survivors. Many rape victims acknowledge that they feel changed by what happened, including feeling a diminishment of sexual desire. Some fear they have been rendered sexually unresponsive by the rape. Very young and sexually inexperienced victims can be so traumatized by the assault that they may develop a long-term fear of sex. For others, the emotions associated with the attack mix with all the other challenges of daily life and complicate or undermine the impulse toward having sex. Anxiety associated with engaging in sexual intimacy, reduced arousal, lack of desire, and an overall decline in sexual satisfaction are commonly reported by victims, often for an extended period.

This chapter focuses on how rape affects post-assault sexual behaviors. It describes patterns of sexual dysfunction that can emerge because of rape and explains how victims struggle to cope with their concerns about physical intimacy. It also addresses the complex ways that men may respond if their intimate partner is raped, including both maladaptive and adaptive responses. Finally, this chapter offers strategies to reduce sexual fears and restore healthy sexual outcomes for victims and their partners. Although the information provided focuses on heterosexual relationships, it is applicable to intimate nonheterosexual relationships as well.

THE VARIOUS CAUSES AND FORMS OF SEXUAL DYSFUNCTION

What are some of the causes and possible consequences of post-assault sexual responsiveness among rape victims? The answer depends on a number of factors that can shape how each rape survivor responds, including the victim's age, her relationship to the perpetrator, the nature and extent of her physical injuries, the circumstances under which the assault occurred, and her mental state before and after the assault.

The interactions she has with others following the assault form the general mindset regarding how she will address concerns about sexual intimacy. Despite individual differences in sensitivity or responsiveness to sexual activity, there are several post-assault patterns that are common to many rape survivors.

Physical Injury

An important consideration for sexual responsiveness involves the nature and extent of physical injury caused by the rape. Included here could be any combination of the following:

- Genital injury, especially if penetration involved the use of objects or multiple assailants

- Genital mutilation

- Sexually transmitted infection

- Chronic pelvic pain

- Pregnancy, including termination of pregnancy

- Persistent genital pain that occurs during intercourse

- Fractures, lacerations, or other significant injuries

For many rape victims, some degree of physical injury occurs during the assault. The nature and extent of such physical injuries reinforce the basic need for her to receive immediate medical attention. In some cases, post-assault corrective surgery or medication is needed. The time required to heal will vary. During this healing period, any attempt to resume sexual intimacy is both ill-advised and likely to complicate intimate relations for an even longer period.

Flashbacks

Although various physical injuries take time to heal, the emotional scars left behind may, in the long run, have the greatest effect on a victim's sexual responsiveness. Among the most common negative consequences for many victims is when intimacy with a partner unexpectedly triggers a flashback of the rape itself. Such flashbacks intrude on one's thoughts and emotions in such a manner as to make sexual activity unappealing and possibly frightening. Triggers typically are situational cues that remind the victim of the assault. The simple truth is that virtually anything present in the environment during the sexual assault could function to trigger a flashback. The following are possible examples of such triggers:

- The smell of alcohol or tobacco

- The scent of cologne

- Certain words (especially words with sexual references)

- A specific song or type of music

- Certain items of clothing

- Common household objects present during the assault

- A particular tone of voice

- Various background noises

How to Recognize Flashbacks

Flashbacks of the rape can occur at any time and may be triggered by an array of objects, situations, or sensory experiences. Flashbacks of the assault are especially common for rape survivors when entering various levels of sexual intimacy. Like the unexpected experience of an electrical shock, the flashback can function to stun the person and place a halt on whatever she was feeling at that moment.

There are clues that can suggest to you she is having a troubling flashback. A significant clue is if there is a sudden shift in her attention, emotional state, or behavior for no clear reason. Additional indicators of a flashback may include a blank stare, hyperventilation, a sudden flood of emotion such as bursting into tears, having what appears to be a panic attack, or simply "freezing up" and scarcely being able to move or communicate. During a flashback, it is as if she is there and present one moment, then abruptly seems disoriented, "lost," or disengaged from whatever is happening. Usually there is no gradual build-up to such disengagement. Rather, it seems to strike with immediacy and urgency, and without an obvious explanation.

Many rape survivors find it difficult to speak about what is happening to them when a flashback happens. They find it especially awkward to say anything if the flashback occurs during an intimate moment. For them in that moment, silence may be preferable than to say anything about very troubling imagery, especially if the imagery contained in the flashback is sexually graphic.

If you strongly suspect she is lost in a flashback, do not touch or shake her to get her to "snap out of it." Such contact at this moment may be incorporated into the flashback experience and enhance its hold on her. Instead, in a calm voice, try to reorient her to her surroundings. Gently tell her that she is safe, that you are with her, and that no harm will come to her. Once she has regained her composure, do not ask her for the details of what she was experiencing, as such a question could take her back into a negative space. Rather, simply ask her what you might do in the future either to help her avoid such an experience or help her get through it without making it more difficult. Let her know that you are willing to alter your behavior or the surroundings if it will help her to avoid such an experience again.

Not only do intrusive memories of the assault decrease sexual responsiveness, but fear that a flashback *might* occur also has a similar effect. In short, both the memory trigger itself and the fear of possibly being triggered can inhibit sexual interactions with a partner. In addition, many rape victims are reluctant to tell their intimate partners that certain stimuli may function as triggers. Some victims may not even know why they are having flashbacks, much less know how to explain to their partners the source of their anxiety. Even if they know exactly what stimulus triggers an unwanted memory, rape victims may decline to say anything out of concern for how it might affect their partners. Although more will be said about this shortly, relationship stress between intimate partners increases in the absence of open communication about sex.

Spectatoring

Another relatively common sexual outcome for women who are victims of rape is a phenomenon called *spectatoring*. This is a form of mental detachment that literally means being a "spectator" during sexual intimacy, rather than being in the moment and experiencing pleasurable sensations. Because rape produces a host of anxieties surrounding sex, many victims are so worried during intimacy that they lose focus. Instead of being emotionally present during sex, in a sense they become observers of their interactions rather than participants.

A woman who is spectatoring is not immersing herself in the positive sensory aspects of the sexual experience with her partner. Instead, she is engaging in an anxious, self-conscious dialog about her body and performance. She may be worried about her appearance, her responsiveness, whether her partner still finds her attractive, whether her partner is experiencing pleasure, whether she might have a flashback, what her partner may be thinking about her responsiveness, or any number of other distracting thoughts.

Although spectatoring also occurs among women who have never been sexually assaulted, the frequency with which it happens to rape victims is significant. Furthermore, a woman who had never engaged in such self-conscious dialog during intimacy before an assault may be shaken at the distractions that now seem to be in her thoughts after an assault. Not only is anxiously watching oneself anything but erotic, it may compel a victim of sexual assault to treat intimate moments as a kind of detached performance. In a genuine desire to please her partner, she may act as if her sexual experience is pleasurable, even if it is not. Faking climax is one example of such a performance.

It is important to understand that sexual anxieties caused by sexual assault generally fade as the recovery process advances. If spectatoring occurs for a victim, this does not mean she will never again experience pleasure during moments of intimacy with her partner. Spectatoring is not a mental disorder, and neither is it a permanent "condition" that inevitably impairs a person's ability to enjoy sex. Whether the issue is flashbacks, spectatoring, or other fears surrounding sex, the critical thing for partners to do is to communicate openly about what is happening regarding their intimate lives. Again, more will be said about this shortly.

Risky Sexual Activity

There is another significant sexual consequence of rape that seems counterintuitive. Instead of a decline or lack of interest in sexual conduct, a minority of rape victims become highly sexually active in ways that can be problematic. Typically, this involves women in their teens or early twenties who behave in sexually risky ways after being raped, such as engaging in casual sex with a series of partners but without any meaningful emotional involvement. Whatever one may choose to call it—callous sex, angry sex, indifferent sex, power sex, or casual hookups—this behavior has its roots in the trauma of sexual assault. It is as if such sexual activity somehow is meant to compensate for what was taken from the rape victim. Very likely there are multiple reasons why some women choose this course of action, which may include a desire to:

- feel wanted or "loved."

- feel attractive.

- gain approval or social acceptance.

- gain self-esteem.

- reduce feelings of disconnection or loneliness.

- feel in control.

- have power over men.

- replace memories of the assault with other sexual experiences.

- "get even" with a perpetrator who is a former partner.

- prove that one is still capable of sexual engagement despite the assault.

- prove that one is not "damaged goods."

- numb one's emotional pain.

This list of reasons is not exhaustive and could easily go on. It is a mistake, however, to dismiss this behavior as disreputable promiscuity rooted in a character flaw. Rather, the important point is that such a pattern of sexual behavior is a way of coping with trauma. For many, it is a way to regain the power over one's sexuality, which may feel as though it were stolen during the rape. The problem, of course, is that risky sexual behaviors can also increase the chances of further harm. For example, there is a high correlation between heavy drinking, "hooking up" in unsafe situations, and being sexually victimized again. On the positive side, such experimentation with risky sexual behaviors generally does not persist over a long period of time. Recovery is a journey. Even if risky experimentation occurs for some along the way, with support most survivors change course and realize that they are fully capable of healthy sexual lives.

Future Romantic Involvement

There is one additional challenge facing rape survivors with respect to their intimate lives. Because most rapes involve adolescent and young adult women, there are consequences that can affect their future romantic relationships with men. Consider as an example an eighteen- or nineteen-year-old student who is raped by someone she met at a party during her first year of college. How might this event influence her willingness to risk entering future romantic relationships with men? What relationship challenges will she face? In what ways does the fact that she is a rape survivor shape how men may view her, or she them?

For each new potential romantic partner that may enter her life in the years to come, she is likely to face an array of apprehensions about how deep to go in the relationship. These apprehensions can be illustrated by the kinds of questions she may ask herself each time she enters and progresses in a relationship, which may include the following:

- Can I trust him?

- Is he an honest and caring person, or someone who is capable of hurting women?

- What, if anything, should I say to him about what happened to me?

- If we become close, am I being dishonest if I do not tell him what happened? Does he have a right to know?

- If I do disclose, how will he respond?

- How should I respond if he does not react well to my disclosure?

- If I tell him about the rape, will he think of me as "damaged"? Will he blame me?

- If this relationship moves toward becoming sexual, should I tell him why I may be reluctant? Will he think I am rejecting him because of what another person did to me?

- Am I even capable of having an intimate relationship?

Clearly, rape can influence the willingness of a survivor to form romantic relationships, including intimate ones, long after the assault. Apprehensions about disclosure, about sexual engagement, and about the trustworthiness of potential partners form the background against which her decisions must be navigated. It is not known how many rape survivors simply avoid romantic relationships altogether, or perhaps feel they are unworthy or incapable of an intimate relationship. And it is not known how many rape survivors continue to struggle with connecting emotionally and physically with good men long after the assault. But what is known is hopeful. Honest and open communication built upon trust can overcome difficulties for *both* parties in an intimate relationship. For a man, knowing how to respond properly to a partner's sexual and related concerns caused by a rape is a critical step in building that trust.

GUIDELINES FOR INTIMATE PARTNERS

If you are the intimate partner of a rape victim at the time of the assault, a disruption in sexual activity following the attack is likely. How long this disruption may last will vary, and may depend, in part, on how you respond to her needs and concerns. Difficulties in the resumption of sexual intimacy may be especially acute if the rape was extremely violent or sadistic, involved multiple rapists, or caused significant injuries. As previously indicated, physical pain, flashbacks, or other fears surrounding sex may now intrude on the intimate life of partners, compounding difficulties in sexual responsiveness. In addition, if relationship problems existed prior to the assault, they may be aggravated by the disruption in sexual intimacy.

It is common for both parties in an intimate relationship to experience uncertainties and complex feelings about the resumption of sex following rape. If you are unobservant or insensitive to her concerns, engaging in sexual activity before she is ready may unintentionally result in her being reminded of the assault. As a man who loves her, ask yourself a basic question: What can I do to help her to regain a sense of control over sexual decision making? The simple answer is to communicate honestly and take your cues from her. This means there are several things you should and should not do to reestablish a positive intimate relationship.

- Do not pressure her into sexual activity before she is ready. Some men believe that the early resumption of sex is a way to normalize the relationship or help her to recover. A return to sexual activity may seem like a behavioral indicator that things are back to normal, even if they are not. You may think to yourself, "Now that we are sexually intimate again, she must be okay." She may even consent to the resumption of sex before she is ready because she wants to please you.

- One indication that she may be conflicted is if she seems to tolerate your touch but is passive and does not answer to it. If she is not ready to resume sexual relations, the act of lovemaking may diminish her sexual desire and complicate your relationship. Honest communication about whether she truly is ready to resume making love is essential. Let her be the guide.

- Just as you should not pressure her into an early resumption of sex, neither should you avoid any display of affection. Understandably, you may assume she feels a diminished interest in sex and step back from her out of consideration. Yet it is important that she not interpret your behavior as a sign you feel she is "tarnished" by the rape or less appealing than before. Many victims fear their partners will see them as "tainted" by the rape. There are ways to express affection (e.g., hugging, handholding, nonsexual massage) without engaging in sexual activity. For example, asking permission to cuddle with her demonstrates affection and gives her control over how to respond.

- Remember that certain cues can be triggers that produce flashbacks of the assault and inhibit sexual responsiveness. Acknowledge that sexually graphic flashbacks and even panic attacks regarding intimacy do not mean that her capacity for a healthy and pleasurable sexual relationship is shattered. Reassure her that you know the occurrence of flashbacks is a common but temporary consequence of rape.

- Her ability to talk about flashbacks can reduce her vulnerability to them. Tell her that if she wishes, you will listen in a nonjudgmental way to any information she feels able to discuss. A willingness to talk honestly, and a commitment to alter patterns associated with intimacy, will be reassuring and help to reduce her sexual fears.

- Although honest communication with her about intimacy is essential, there is one thing you should guard against discussing. Some men involuntarily experience sexual arousal when a victim of rape describes what was done to her and then feel guilty for having such a response. This suggests just how emotionally confusing rape can be. If you do feel aroused when she describes what happened, *do not* communicate this to her. Such a confusing message would only provoke more anxiety in her. If such feelings persist, however, then it would be helpful for you to seek the assistance of a counselor.

- Never suggest that you view the rapist as a sexual rival. Never suggest that you think women have a secret desire to be "taken" and forced by a rapist to perform sexual acts. Never suggest that she may have enjoyed the rape experience. Never ask if she experienced an orgasm during the rape. If these are recurring thoughts, it is best to speak with a counselor.

- Two of the most important things you can do are both simple and difficult. First, ask her to give you guidance on what she does or does not want in terms of levels of intimacy before initiating anything physical. Let her know that if she is reluctant, confused, anxious, or even unsure of what she wants in a sexual sense, you will respect her uncertainty and be content simply to be present with her. Let her know that you will not place on her any subtle pressure or expect physical intimacy until she is clear on what she wants and communicates it to you.

  Second, admit to her your own vulnerability—that you also feel anxious, confused, and uncertain about how to navigate the emotionally complex terrain of sex since the rape. Tell her that you do not want to do anything that may cause her harm, and that you will let her take the lead. The more she feels that you understand her state of mind, and the more she feels that you are willing to let her progress on her terms and at a pace comfortable to her, the better the chances will be of regaining a healthy intimate relationship.

- Do not become angry with her or assume she is rejecting you if she is less sexually responsive than before. Neither should you doubt your adequacy as a man or feel insecure about her diminished responsiveness. Her post-assault reluctance is not about your suitability as her partner, but rather a consequence of trauma. You are not the reason for the temporary disruption in your intimate life as a couple. Be patient. Trust that with sensitivity and a willingness to let her proceed at her own pace, intimacy will return.

- As a couple, if problems about sexual concerns become a source of anger, bitterness, or deepening misunderstanding, relationship counseling is highly recommended. Your willingness to seek counseling together is not a measure of failure, but an expression of commitment to the relationship. Articulating powerful feelings to someone professionally equipped to address relationship tensions will help both of you find what may feel lost.

Later Relationships

At the onset of a romance, as trust builds, couples generally share with one another significant experiences from their pasts. Revealing a prior experience of sexual victimization, however, is an especially complex challenge for both the woman and her new partner. If you are a man who enters a romance with a woman who was sexually assaulted years before, how should you respond if she tells you about the rape? How should you respond if she does not tell you, but you have a strong suspicion that she may have been sexually victimized? What concerns might each of you have as your relationship unfolds?

Whenever a woman decides to disclose that she was raped, that decision is both an act of courage and an act of trust. It is courageous because of misunderstandings and negative judgments about victims that permeate our society. Disclosure is an act of trust because she is making herself vulnerable to the uncertainties of how another person may respond. Disclosure risks opening old wounds and anxieties, but it can also strengthen the bonds between two people depending on the response.

As a caring man, if you are at a point in a relationship where a woman reveals she was sexually assaulted at an earlier time in her life, your first response is likely to be both shock and uncertainty. You are likely to recognize this as a pivotal moment in your relationship and fear that any misstep on your part will cause harm or be a problem. You are likely to be flooded with questions but do not know what to ask or how to ask them. And you are likely to wonder if you are equipped to handle whatever relationship complexities may emerge out of this revelation.

Although her disclosure of rape is unexpected, know that this is something she has lived with and processed for many months or years. In other words, you and she are at different points of understanding. The fact that she has divulged this to you suggests that she is perhaps advanced in her recovery as a rape survivor. You, however, may experience the acute emotional reactions her family members or close friends experienced when the rape occurred. These reactions may include anger, a desire for justice, confusion, uncertainty, anxiety, or other emotional responses. Your initial response to her disclosure can set the tone for what happens in the relationship.

Negative Responses

There is a limited body of research on how men address disclosures of rape if the assault occurred much earlier in the lives of victims. Rape survivors indicate that there are two general types of male response that are hurtful and can undermine the continuation of a relationship. The first category of poor response is if the man seems to blame her for what happened. For example, asking her what she did that "caused" the perpetrator to act as he did. Any questioning that shames her or is harshly judgmental of her conduct at the time of the assault is an inappropriate response to her disclosure. Any suggestion that she is damaged because she was raped is inappropriate. Furthermore, if he only seems interested in the sexual aspects of the rape and disinterested in the impact it has had on her life, then that is a good indication of his insensitivity. If such are his responses, he has done her a great dis-service by violating her trust, and he has likely damaged the emerging relationship beyond repair.

The second type of response is perhaps more complex for a survivor to navigate. In this case, the man indicates he has no idea how to respond to the disclosure, almost as if it is too great a burden for him to deal with and process. From her point of view, such a reaction may cause the man to appear indifferent, disengaged, or callous, as though he views the subject as something he would rather not discuss. In a trusting way, she has just revealed something momentous in her life and then she draws a blank response. Now what should she do? Try to educate him about rape and its consequences? Ask him to explain his reaction after he just indicated he does not know how to respond? Does she feel terrible for mentioning it and "burdening" him? Does this silence her?

Positive Responses

What is a better male response, one that can build upon her trust and strengthen communication? Here are a few suggestions:

- Acknowledge it took courage for her to disclose this experience.

- Thank her for caring enough to trust you with this information.

- Ask her if she is willing to answer some questions you have. If the answer is yes, then begin by asking her about how well she is doing since the rape occurred. Ask her if she will share some of the challenges she has faced during her recovery. And ask her how she has grown because of her struggle to recover. These questions are good starting points for further discussion.

- Acknowledge that although you may not have much experience dealing with sexual violence, you are willing to listen without judgment to whatever she wishes to discuss about what happened.

- Tell her you are willing to be a support person in any remaining struggles she has as a rape survivor.

Such responses will set the stage for open communication and serve as a basis to develop mutual understanding. As trust builds, expect that the topic of what happened to her will unfold over the course of more than one conversation (unless she indicates she does not want to have further discussions). The strategies for effective communication discussed earlier in this book can serve as a guide.

UNSPOKEN ISSUES

There is a flip side to the rape disclosure process, one that poses a different challenge for a man. In the progression of a new relationship, as emotional bonds begin to deepen, sometimes it seems as if the developing connection suddenly hits a wall. It may seem as if a female partner shifts direction or becomes more distant without explanation. What he thought was positive signaling from her about becoming close may abruptly change to neutral or even go in reverse. To be forthright, this often occurs around issues of physical intimacy, though it is not limited to this subject. Given the high number of young women who are sexually victimized in their teenage years (often by someone they trusted), it is no surprise that many will feel conflicted as they enter a new relationship. Issues of trust, intimacy, self-esteem, and related matters from the rape can surface. And if a man is a careful and caring observer, he may suspect the change in a partner's behavior reflects the fact that she was sexually traumatized.

If a man suspects his new companion was raped and she has not disclosed this information, what should he do? If the relationship has hit a wall, it does neither party any good to pretend that nothing is wrong. It is worth the risk to gently raise a concern and give the other person a chance to explain. To raise a concern is not to make an accusation. It is to gently create an opening to deepen communication. The man may approach his concern by saying, "I care about you, and I would like our relationship to continue to grow. Recently, though, it seems as if you may be concerned about something that could be uncomfortable to discuss. I do know that many women have had bad experiences with men before, and that these experiences can carry over into new relationships. If there is something you are willing to talk about, I promise to listen and be supportive. I just want to understand and be of help."

One should not force disclosure or necessarily assume a traumatic history if the relationship shifts. At the least, however, it is important to give her a chance to say what is on her mind. The risk of creating a sincere opening for discussion outweighs the risk of remaining silent. As always, however, it is her choice whether to disclose.

CONCLUSION

There is no magic formula to resolve the many sexual issues associated with rape. The residue of emotions surrounding sexuality left by an attack can become embedded in all aspects of a rape survivor's life, including relations with current and future intimate partners. The one common denominator for the restoration of healthy outcomes is the opportunity to talk freely and honestly about how rape trauma plays into a survivor's sex life. Acknowledging conflicts, fears, hopes, and feelings about intimacy is one essential ingredient for the restoration of sexual health. The other essential ingredient is patience expressed through unconditional caring. With these ingredients in place, trust that what was stolen by the act of rape can be returned and made even stronger.

6.

Parental Concerns During the Recovery Process

The rape or sexual abuse of a minor (i.e., a preteen or young adolescent) most often involves a perpetrator who is known and trusted by the victim. Any combination of force, deception, trickery, coercion, scare tactics, false kindness, bribery, and abuse of authority can be used by a perpetrator to manipulate a victim. Using this type of manipulation, an abuser intentionally encroaches on a potential victim's physical and psychological spaces to see how she might react to sexual advances—"testing the waters," so to speak—in a process known as *grooming*. This process may include special gifts, offers to befriend and help the young person, and declarations of how "special" their relationship is, which also emphasize the notion of keeping secrets. Although a comprehensive discussion of the sexual victimization of very young children is beyond the scope of this book, it is important to understand that when a very young person has been violated physically and psychologically, she has likely been lied to by her perpetrator, whom she may have trusted, and made to feel responsible for the sexual violation, and probably blames herself for what happened.

In general, the longer the duration of abuse and the closer the perpetrator is to the victim or her family, the more severe the emotional turmoil. A victim's age, level of social and physical development, relationship to the perpetrator, and life experiences, as well as the nature, extent, and duration of abuse are all important factors that will shape how both she and her parents address this traumatic experience. The younger the victim, the less likely she will have developed the knowledge and coping skills required to build a solid foundation for her recovery. Although the primary emphasis of this book is on how men can help adolescent

81

and adult females who have been sexually assaulted, the guidance in this chapter is relevant to parents of a victim who is a minor. It therefore is essential for a father and mother to understand the stresses on their child in the days and weeks after an assault, and to be positive guides throughout the recovery process.

Before identifying the concerns that are likely to arise when a minor is sexually assaulted, it is necessary to first acknowledge a dilemma that both parents will likely face. Experts in rape recovery emphasize the importance of empowering the victim. Fundamentally, this means encouraging a rape victim to regain control over her life, including letting her make her own decisions and not dictating what she should or should not do as she recovers. This book strongly endorses such an approach to empowerment. That said, there are difficult questions to consider. When a victim is a preteen or young adolescent still under the protection and authority of her parents, what form should empowerment take? What decisions should she make, and what decisions should be the responsibility of the parents? Is it appropriate for parents to compel their daughter to follow a course of action if she resists it? Who is in the better position to know what is in the best interests of the minor, her or her parents? If conflicts over what to do arise, how should they be resolved?

Even professionals working in the field of rape may not agree on how to address all the concerns that can emerge when a minor has been sexually victimized. This is especially true if a perpetrator is a sibling, stepsibling, or other family member. Because of the unique family environment and other circumstances surrounding each case, approaches to recovery most likely will vary and need to be individualized to some degree.

There are, however, two general points on which nearly all professionals agree. First, if there are two parents actively involved in raising a child who has been sexually victimized, both need to be on the same page and consistent in their communications with her. Conflict between parents on what to do will inevitably create tension with their child. Even if a child's parents are divorced, they need to find a way to work together to help their daughter. Second, the sexual victimization of a minor creates so many challenges within a family that the need for outside professional guidance is nearly always a necessity. Whether this guidance involves some form of family therapy or other counseling approach, a third-party professional who can work with all members of a household is one of the most important resources available. Assuming that both parents are in agreement on what to do and have access to professional help, there are additional guidelines for them to consider.

GUIDELINES FOR FATHERS AND MOTHERS

For a significant number of young females, coerced sexual encounters, including rape and child sexual abuse, are their first "sexual" experiences. If forced intercourse or another form of sexual abuse was your daughter's first "sexual" experience, then it likely created in her a fear of sex and had negative consequences on her understanding of human intimacy. It also likely produced feelings of shame, guilt, and embarrassment in her, as well as fearful concerns about her reputation, all of which adversely affected her self-esteem. Despite her youth, she was thrust into a complex adult world of cruel sexuality, violence, deception, psychological manipulation, and possibly legal entanglements before she was developmentally ready to navigate it. As a result, this experience may produce in her (and in her parents) deep feelings of grief over what may be called "the sadness of innocence lost." Your tasks as a parent are the following:

- Clarify her fears and misunderstandings about sexual intimacy.

- Strive to reduce her feelings of shame and guilt.

- Help to restore her self-esteem.

- Minimize conflicts that may arise because of her victimization.

- Help her to return to the normalcy of being a child or young adolescent.

What She Needs to Know

Given her young age, your daughter needs several clear and consistent messages from you. She needs to know that rape (or sexual molestation) is a crime of violence and not an act of "uncontrolled passion." She needs to know that she bears no responsibility for the actions of the perpetrator, even if he made her think what happened was her fault. Make it clear that what was done to her is not how loving couples express themselves sexually or emotionally. Communicate to her that she has not been tarnished by this traumatic experience, and that her capacity to have loving relationships in the future has not been diminished.

She may be concerned that the sexual assault constitutes the loss of her virginity. Even if she is too embarrassed or cannot find the words to articulate this concern to you, the sadness she likely feels in this regard is something that needs to be addressed. Explain to her that there is a profound difference between giving oneself freely in a loving way to another person and being sexually assaulted. Because what happened to her was not consensual, she should consider her virginity intact in every meaningful way.

If she has had one or more highly sexualized traumatic experiences inflicted upon her, it is normal for her to have questions about many

A Word to Fathers

Most fathers have an acute sense of responsibility for the safety of their daughters who have yet to reach adulthood. It is therefore not surprising that a father might feel that he has failed in his duty as a protector if his daughter has been the target of sexual assault. Similarly, it is not surprising that a common response when a father learns his daughter has been victimized is deep anger at this injustice and a forceful desire to take action against the perpetrator. The intensity of his response can be so powerful that it actually makes his daughter's recovery more difficult by adding another fear to her struggle: the fear of what her father *might* do.

Although a daughter may entertain any number of fears regarding her father's possible responses to her assault, the following examples are the most common:

● Fear she caused her father to "lose it" and be out of control

● Fear her father will take the law into his own hands

● Fear her father will interrogate her friends who may know the circumstances surrounding the assault

● Fear her father will deny her access to her friends

● Fear her father will directly contact the perpetrator or his parents aspects of human sexuality. As a parent, however, you may find it uncomfortable having frank discussions with her about sex. Similarly, she may be reluctant or too embarrassed to voice her questions to you, especially if she believes you feel the topic is taboo. Admittedly, such open discussions about sex can be awkward for a child and her parents. Nevertheless, a hesitancy to provide information about human sexuality when that information is sought by the victim is counterproductive in several ways. First, it suggests that what she experienced is too awful to discuss and implies that she must figure it out on her own. Second, a lack of information will likely heighten her fears about sex, including anxieties that she may have been damaged sexually because of what happened. Finally, a lack of adult guidance regarding her questions

- Fear her father will demand school officials do something that she will find embarrassing

- Fear her father will either restrict her freedoms or engage in excessive surveillance of her activities

- Fear her father and mother will argue about what they should do to help her

- Fear her relationship with her father will deteriorate

- Fear that talking about the assault will anger her father

However understandable it may be for a father to feel the need to take charge and act decisively following the sexual assault of his daughter, caution is required. He may unintentionally be pitting his need to act against her need for predictability and emotional security. In a sense, a father's role should be primarily passive. He should strive to see the world from her vantage point and give her choices. This requires him to keep in check the impulses telling him to act in ways that may create fear in her. To put it another way, a father should communicate to his daughter a kind of reverse action plan, in which he lets her know what he will not do as a measure of his support. Quelling her fears in this manner avoids conflicts and hastens her recovery.

about sex may compel her to find answers from problematic sources, which may include pornography.

It is critically important that she is encouraged to ask any questions about sex and be given honest answers. As a parent, if you are simply too uncomfortable or feel unable to provide such information, a sympathetic and knowledgeable person such as a counselor or medical professional should be available to answer her questions. In addition, she should have the option of being given age-appropriate written materials that can help her to frame questions, find answers, and understand the terminology used to discuss human sexuality. Finally, sexual assault can raise questions in a young victim's thoughts about her sexual identity. If such questions arise, she may not be willing to share them with you. Again, she will benefit from the opportunity to discuss her concerns with a knowledgeable and sympathetic person who can give her guidance. Responding honestly and helping her to find answers will reduce her fears and aid in her recovery.

If she was assaulted by an acquaintance or someone she was dating, she needs to know she is not responsible for causing him to "lose control." Demonstrations of affection or friendship on her part do not make her liable for his actions. In addition, she needs to understand that her assailant is not representative of all men, that other men can be worthy of her trust, and that trust is an essential part of a healthy relationship.

Your daughter may be concerned about what others may be saying about her on social media. If she becomes the object of gossip or even personal attacks by her peers, discuss with her whether or not she should respond, and what strategy to take if she does. In some instances, it may be necessary to secure legal guidance if someone persists in posting hurtful information.

Parent-Daughter Communication Challenges

If tensions in communication between you and your daughter existed prior to the rape, then an assault is likely to compound these communication problems. When such tensions are present, many adolescent victims do not want to share what happened with their parents. In this case, a refusal to disclose is not about a victim being deliberately defiant. More likely it is about her fear of being misunderstood, punished, or seen as responsible for what happened, or of losing freedoms.

If your daughter decides not to discuss the details of the assault, do not try to force her to discuss them. Do not threaten to remove privileges unless she talks about what happened. Do not claim that you have a right to know as a parent. This is not a contest of wills. Disclosure is an important part of recovery, but only if it is given voluntarily and emerges out of a need to make sense of the assault and gain support. A better option would be to acknowledge from the start that it is her choice to discuss what happened on her terms whenever she is ready. You are there to listen, not to judge her conduct.

If you avoid ever talking about the assault, it may give your daughter the impression that you are ashamed and hold her responsible. Let her know that you are neither angry with her nor ashamed of her behavior. If she does not want to share any details with you, then provide her with the option of speaking with a counselor. Do not to turn the matter into a major conflict, but rather reinforce the idea that she can benefit from talking about this traumatic experience, provided it is her decision to do so.

If your daughter consumed alcohol or drugs (perhaps at a social gathering or with a date) and then was raped, she will probably fear that you will hold her responsible for being disobedient and reckless. She may fear punishment. She may fear that you will act in ways that will embarrass her. She may fear that you will think she brought it on herself. In anticipation of your negative responses, she may deny having used drugs or alcohol, or simply conceal this information from you. Doing so, however, may escalate into a conflict with you as her parent, which will work against her recovery. Caution should be taken not to focus on the use of drugs or alcohol instead of the sexual violence. As a parent, your first concern is to help her recover from the assault. To avoid a distracting conflict, let her know that even if her use of drugs or alcohol is upsetting to you, there will be no punishment. Communicate that your primary concern is to be supportive as she deals with the trauma of the assault.

If you know your daughter has experimented with drugs or alcohol, then it is prudent to carefully monitor her for an escalation in use after the assault. The risk of self-medication often increases following a rape and should be strongly discouraged. If you learn that your daughter is using drugs or alcohol to cope, consult with professionals who know how to address the complexities of both adolescent substance abuse and sexual victimization.

It is sometimes the case that an adolescent rape survivor will use her victimization as leverage to inappropriately manipulate her parents. This can be true whether her parents are together or divorced. Admittedly, it is a delicate balancing act for parents who want to be supportive yet are being pushed to consider things that are contrary to their best judgment. Although some disruption in daily routines following an assault is to be expected, over the long run parents need to find a delicate balance in holding reasonable expectations for their daughter during her recovery. Allowing her to skip school, not do homework, avoid household chores, argue with siblings, stay out late with friends, or do other things not ordinarily permitted should not become points of negotiation. She needs to know that although you love and support her recovery, you are consistent in your expectations and have not relinquished your role as a parent.

Sibling Sexual Abuse

Sibling or stepsibling sexual abuse is the most common form of sexual victimization to occur within families. The abuser typically is a juvenile (most often a male) who targets a younger sibling or stepsibling (most often a preteen female). The sexualized behavior is age-inappropriate, not motivated by normal curiosity about sex, initiated without consent, reflective of a power differential between the perpetrator and the victim, done in secret, and usually repeated.

A victim of sibling sexual abuse is often unwilling to reveal to her parents what happened. She may simultaneously feel betrayed by her older sibling yet protective of him. Very likely she has been coerced by her older sibling into keeping "their secret" and understands what the consequences for the family will be as a result of disclosure. She may have been told that she will be responsible for breaking up the family if she talks about the secret. Often a parent discovers what happened by chance and then faces the dilemma of how to address the consequences. The divided loyalties inevitably associated with such a betrayal are like a shock wave that sweeps through the entire family. If there are conflicting accounts of what transpired, then some family members may take sides,

There could be a decline in your daughter's school performance following an assault. Once again, as a parent you must strike a delicate balance between making sure she performs well in school even as you help her work through the emotional challenges involved in her recovery. If she begins to suffer academic difficulties related to the assault, you will be faced with a dilemma and a potential source of conflict. Your daughter may want the assault to remain confidential, but if her grades are suffering, should school officials be informed of what happened? Generally, schools will make accommodations for students under special circumstances. But if your daughter is not performing well and school officials are unaware that her difficulties are related to sexual assault, she will be saddled with the consequences of low or failing grades. She also risks being perceived negatively by her teachers, who may think she is simply not trying hard enough or doesn't care.

especially if the assault involves blended families with a stepsibling as the perpetrator.

Although a full consideration of sibling sexual abuse goes well beyond the focus of this book, parents need to understand a basic message: In the absence of professional intervention, this type of abuse has the capacity to divide family members and destroy family relationships. As difficult as it may be, parents who learn of this abuse have an obligation to bring it to the attention of professionals, perhaps at a rape crisis center or through child protective services. These professionals can offer guidance on questions about possible police involvement as well as therapeutic options for the family. A safety plan will need to be established, and counseling for both the victim and the perpetrator will be required.

If your daughter has been the target of sibling sexual abuse, she most likely feels confused and partially responsible for the turmoil in the family. She needs to know that she did not cause this turmoil. She needs to understand the inappropriate and harmful nature of her sibling's actions, and that what happened was not her fault. Your response to her (and to everyone else) should be clear: Her recovery takes priority over the perpetrator's position in the family. Your duty as a parent is clear: Support your child and explain the inappropriate nature of the perpetrator's actions.

The desire to respect your daughter's confidentiality must be tempered with the need to safeguard her academic success. School officials have a legal obligation to maintain confidentiality regarding matters of student health. If you wish to inform school personnel, however, do not do so without first discussing the matter with your daughter. Explain to her that sharing information with school officials on a "need to know" basis is a reasonable course of action. If she resists this idea, the guidance and recommendation of her counselor should be sought. She needs to understand that teachers and school counselors can modify academic tasks and provide support that will help her to succeed in school while she navigates her recovery.

Encourage your daughter to resume her normal lifestyle without being overly protective. Limiting your daughter's growing independence, or even grounding her for not being sufficiently careful, would be counterproductive and could be a source of resentment. It is important that her rights regarding seeing friends and playing sports, involvement in extracurricular activities at school, and responsibility for household duties remain intact.

If you learn that your adolescent daughter has been raped, it is imperative that she undergo a medical exam. The risk of genital injury or other injuries, sexually transmitted infections, and pregnancy necessitate medical attention. Gently convince your daughter of the need for a medical exam and make certain any procedures she may undergo are explained in advance by a medical professional. Give her the option of having a trusted person accompany her through the exam if she wishes. Most often a young victim will cooperate.

But what if she does not want to cooperate, even though she is a minor? To be honest, this is a grey area where not everyone agrees. As her a parent, you still have authority over her and can compel her to take the exam. If law enforcement is involved, they too can exert pressure on you to require your daughter to take a medical exam. If your daughter is hesitant to take a medical exam, then a counselor or victim advocate should be consulted. The bottom line, however, is this: The long-term risk of not receiving medical attention outweighs the temporary risk of upsetting a victim by going against her wishes.

CONCLUSION

The character and duration of your daughter's recovery may rest upon your ability as a parent to juggle all the forces affecting her, you, and your family. There may be times when you will need to trust your parental instincts about what is in your daughter's best interests, even if she does not agree with you. There may be times when you will need to back down so as not to be drawn into conflict with her. There may be times when you will need to trust in her resilience and ability to receive truths despite her youth. There may be times when she will need to rely on your strength and protection, and times when you should not be overprotective of her. There may be times when you will need to accept the guidance of outside professionals. Finally, there may be times when you will need to navigate between her needs and the needs of others in your family. None of this will be easy.

Remember that you are in this for the long haul. What you say and do in the weeks and months following the assault can affect not only your daughter's recovery but also the nature of your relationship with her over time. Remain patient and steadfast in your support. The one constant message that should form the background against which all other communications follow is this: You love her without conditions and will stand by her—and nothing will change this fact.

7.

Non-Stranger Sexual Assault

There is solid evidence indicating that at least one in six women will be the victim of rape or attempted rape. Approximately 80 percent of victims will be under the age of thirty, with teens and college-age women (ages sixteen through twenty-four) being at highest risk. Well over half of sexual assaults occur during these years. The overwhelming majority of them involve perpetrators and victims who know each other.

Although some people use terms such as "acquaintance rape" or "date rape" to describe this type of sexual assault, "non-stranger sexual assault" is the preferred designation because it covers a wider range of possible social connections between perpetrators and victims. Non-strangers may include casual acquaintances, fellow students, coworkers, dating partners, current or former intimate partners, friends, family members, and people met during brief encounters, especially at social gatherings.

In cases where a perpetrator and a victim know one another (either briefly or well), the assault occurs within the context of an interpersonal relationship in which boundaries regarding sexual consent can be confused. This confusion works to the perpetrator's advantage, in that it is easier to mask or deny the assault and avoid detection. Making sense of how non-stranger assault unfolds requires an understanding of how perpetrators employ various forms of coercion, manipulation, deception, denial, gaslighting, abuse of trust, and possibly force to target their victims. Understanding the dynamics of non-stranger assault also requires avoiding preconceptions about victim credibility and how a victim may respond if assaulted by someone with whom she has a social connection. This chapter addresses the legal, social, psychological, and emotional complexities associated with non-stranger sexual assault.

THE PROBLEM OF VICTIM CREDIBILITY

Sexual assault perpetrated by a person known to the victim does not necessarily conform to the stereotype of what many people believe happens during and after a rape. In most cases, no weapon is used, and typically there is an absence of physical violence or threats of violence. Victims generally do not offer physical resistance and usually exhibit little or no obvious physical injury. In addition, many victims are friendly to their perpetrators and acknowledge that they liked or were attracted to them and trusted them. In many instances, victims engaged in consensual intimacy to some degree before the rape. Often they feel some responsibility for what happened. It also is common for victims to feel confusion about whether the actions of their perpetrators should be defined as criminal. Finally, relatively few victims of non-stranger rape report what happened to law enforcement or campus officials. Even if they do decide to report the incident, they do so weeks, months, or even years after it occurred. Such delays call into question a victim's credibility. A victim may not want to involve police or school officials for any number of reasons, which may include:

- not wanting to get the perpetrator in trouble.

- being ashamed, embarrassed, and uncertain about what happened.

- being concerned about what others might think.

- not wanting to explain her interactions with the perpetrator leading up to the assault (e.g., her use of drugs or alcohol).

- having positive feelings toward the perpetrator.

- believing she was at least partially responsible for what happened.

- not wanting to deal with the hassle of police involvement.

- not having a clear recollection of what happened.

- wanting to protect parents or others from getting upset.

- fearing what the perpetrator might say about her conduct or alleged willingness to have sex.

- believing her claim of sexual assault would not be seen as credible.

- being economically dependent or dependent in some other way on the perpetrator.

This last point about victim credibility requires further explanation. A significant percentage of non-stranger sexual assaults happen to members of marginalized groups, who are often seen as less credible by police and others. These marginalized groups include homeless or runaway youth, persons engaged in the sex trade, victims of human trafficking, drug-addicted young women, undocumented workers, transgender women, women of color, persons with police records, and persons with physical or mental disabilities. It is both unfortunate and unfair that a person's perceived status can undermine her account of sexual assault.

The simple truth is that false reports of rape are rare, including among marginalized women. In fact, too often an actual instance of rape is mislabeled as unfounded. Although the problem of mistaken false reports goes beyond the scope of this book, several conclusions are noteworthy regarding this issue. First, mislabeling an actual rape case as false reinforces the negative stereotype that women lie about being sexually assaulted. The greater problem is actually reluctance to report, not false claims of rape. Second, perpetrators are not held accountable and are free to repeat acts of sexual violence. Third, confidence in law enforcement among victims of rape and those who care about them is severely undermined. Finally, the overall willingness of any victim of sexual violence to report the crime or cooperate with police is lessened when law enforcement is known to dismiss reports of rape due to prejudice against victims.

Unfortunately, a victim's credibility in the eyes of law enforcement and others could be called into question due to any number of perfectly normal occurrences in reporting a non-stranger sexual assault. A victim's claim of rape is more likely to be doubted if:

- she exaggerates some details, omits details, or changes details of what happened as she recounts the assault.

- she acknowledges that she did not physically resist the assault.

- she minimizes or does not admit she used drugs or alcohol at the time of the assault.

- she appears calm rather than distressed or upset when she describes the rape.

- she is perceived to be sexually unattractive, perhaps due to weight, disfigurement, blindness, or other characteristics.

- she seems belligerent or hostile when questioned.

- she engaged in some degree of consensual intimacy (e.g., kissing, caressing, modeling for photographs) before the assault.

- she engaged in prior consensual sex with the perpetrator (i.e., they were former intimate partners).

Although false claims of rape are rare, stereotypes about how "real" victims should look, talk, and behave inform how others judge a victim's credibility. Police and others in positions of power, however, should operate under the assumption that a victim has little reason to lie about having been assaulted. If someone expresses vague doubts about a victim's account, seldom can that person articulate a compelling reason for such doubts. Perhaps it is difficult to understand how a woman could be raped by someone with whom she may have been friendly. To better understand non-stranger rape, it is helpful to describe one of the most typical sequences associated with such an assault.

COMMON SEQUENCE OF EVENTS

Unlike sexual assaults perpetrated by strangers, non-stranger rape is best understood as a gradual unfolding of interactions that encroach upon a victim's space rather than a sudden attack. Although it is not possible for this book to review every scenario in which non-stranger sexual assault may occur, it is important to consider the typical situation of many females in high school or college. Their active social lives involve regular attendance at social gatherings where they meet young men with whom there is potential for romantic relationships. In such common encounters, it is normal and understandable for women to be friendly and presume a degree of trust with the men they meet. Unfortunately, this trust and friendliness can be used against them by predatory males who seek opportunities to target women.

A typical sequence of events may unfold as follows: There is a party at which alcohol flows freely and there is peer pressure to drink. It may also include drug use. A young woman encounters a young man with whom she is already acquainted or is meeting for the first time. He encourages her to drink or makes a point of determining if she is already under the influence of alcohol. One of the most common strategies employed by males who perpetrate sexual assault is to "feed drinks" to young women, especially if these women have relatively little experience functioning under the influence. In addition to encouraging a woman to drink, this type of man may flatter her and give her his undivided attention in what, for him, is a subtle game of conquest. Quite simply, he is engaging in a process of gradual desensitization intended to build her trust and determine her vulnerabilities. The ideal target is someone who has been drinking to excess, appears to be trusting, is flattered by attention, and seems to be controllable.

As the target starts to feel the effects of the alcohol, the perpetrator typically tries to separate her from other people and find a room or other private location where they can be alone. He gradually initiates a degree of physical intimacy (e.g., kissing, touching) to which the woman may be responsive. She may even be the one to initiate this level of intimacy. Her consent to this level of intimacy, however, does not mean she has agreed to have sex with him. Nevertheless, he continues to escalate, perhaps by attempting to remove her clothing or by touching her genital areas. Even if she now seems hesitant or uncomfortable with his actions, she may gently try to halt his advances in subtle rather than direct ways. Although her behavior may indicate her discomfort and desire for his actions to cease, she may or may not clearly tell him to stop. She may feel cornered and confused by his persistence, but she may also be reluctant to do something that might "hurt his feelings." Despite her reluctance, he continues his advances without asking for or receiving clear permission to do so. He progressively becomes more insistent, ignoring her lack of desire for a sexual encounter, and ends up "having sex with her" (his interpretation). Although sexual intercourse clearly occurred against her will, he will claim that it was consensual sex.

From the vantage of an opportunistic sexual predator, a woman's consumption of alcohol serves multiple purposes. First, drinking impairs her judgment and compromises her capacity to assess risk. She may find she cannot safely get away from him, particularly if she is relying on him for a ride home. She simply does not have the same degree of freedom to act as he does; he has placed her in a situation in which he is in control. Second, drinking can lead to her having trouble accurately recounting what happened. Blackouts, falling asleep, or not being sure of the exact sequence of events become holes in her narrative. The ambiguities created by drinking allow the predator to offer a counter narrative that is difficult to challenge. Finally, drinking blurs the lines of responsibility, especially if there was some degree of consensual intimacy. This blurriness increases the likelihood that she will appear to have been a willing participant in what the perpetrator and others might claim was a typical "hookup."

The entire setup is designed to convey that this was a consensual sexual encounter, despite her lack of clear consent. Afterward, he may talk to her in a way that suggests he simply followed her lead in the encounter, and that it was a mutually enjoyable intimate experience. He may tell her that he will contact her again for another "date," thus implying that an accepted connection between them now exists. His goal is to confuse her, make her feel a shared responsibility for what happened, and encourage her silence. Simply put: He is gaslighting her. In other words, he is trying to get her to question her own judgment and accept his version of events. If she tells others what happened, he can distort her role in what happened and make it seem as though they both agreed to casual sex. Who could say otherwise? Perpetrator denials in such cases nearly always center on the claim that the sex was consensual.

At the heart of a perpetrator's actions is a deliberate strategy of desensitization, intrusion, deception, manipulation, possible intimidation, and denial. It is an abuse of power, not something created or agreed to by the victim. Her confusion over what transpired, her drinking, and even her acknowledgement that she may have felt attracted to him should not be interpreted as consent. In the absence of her clear consent, his conduct constitutes a sexual assault and should not be thought of as "seduction" or simply a "miscommunication."

In instances such as the one described, most victims do not report the assault to the police or school officials. Those who do face an uphill battle in terms of being believed or seeing their perpetrators face any consequences for their actions. Conflicting claims about consent are at the center of these challenges. Unfortunately, young people live in a

Consent on College Campuses

Given the high rate of non-stranger sexual assault experienced by college-age women, Title IX legislation requires colleges and universities to be more proactive in developing policies and protocols to address the problem, such as creating rape awareness education programs and adopting new disciplinary measures in response to complaints. Many schools have included an "affirmative consent" statement in their policies on sexual assault as a proactive measure.

Essentially, affirmative consent means that all parties must mutually, voluntarily, and explicitly agree, in words or actions, to engage in sexual activity. Participation in such activity cannot be coerced and consent must be unambiguous. Furthermore, consent cannot be given when a person is asleep, unconscious, incapacitated due to alcohol or drug use, or unable to communicate because of a mental or physical condition. Failure to resist physically cannot be interpreted as consent. Silence in the absence of physical indicators of clear willingness to engage sexually cannot be interpreted as consent. To put it simply: Silence is not consent.

The intent behind affirmative consent is to ensure that all parties communicate with one another and receive clear permission before engaging in a sexual encounter. This encourages students to respect each other's boundaries and fosters consensual activities. Sexual contact without permission is prohibited. It also makes clear that any person involved in a sexual act has the right to stop participating in the act at any time and for any reason.

Most colleges and universities with an affirmative consent policy believe that it encourages responsible sexual decision making. In campus disciplinary hearings, participants in a disputed sexual encounter can be questioned about how consent was or was not communicated. Critics of this approach, however, believe that the concept of affirmative consent is overly broad, and that it may not be possible to prove unambiguous consent. Nevertheless, affirmative consent, which states that any person who wishes to engage in sexual activity cannot presume consent in the absence of clear verbal or behavioral indicators, can afford young people on college campuses some form of protection.

world where ideas such as "hookup culture" and "friends with bene-fits" make it seem as if almost any false claim of consensual sex could be credible. This low standard also minimizes the gravity of an unwanted sexual encounter. There is also a widely held—and false—cultural belief that holds a woman accountable for triggering the "natural urges" of a man after having engaged in consensual intimacy such as kissing or fondling to a certain degree. This belief thus places responsibility on women for what may happen to them in these situations. A woman's actions may be seen by others as "implied consent" despite the fact that she did not consent to what happened. It is no wonder that so many victims remain silent rather than expose themselves to others' doubts and judgments.

CONSEQUENCES FOR VICTIMS

Although the effects of non-stranger sexual assault can parallel those of an assault by a stranger, there are some differences between the two. If an attack by a stranger is reported to the police or campus security, generally the report is seen as credible and likely to trigger a serious investigation. An assault by a friend or casual acquaintance creates investigative challenges in gathering corroborating evidence, especially when there are conflicting accounts about consent. Such a situation is more easily dismissed as unfounded. Law enforcement has an obliga-tion to investigate any claim of rape, but the expertise and resources of the police or campus security can vary when addressing a sexual assault associated with young people partying. Too often such cases do not lead to the prosecution of the perpetrators.

If the perpetrator is a current or former intimate partner, there is a tendency to view the reported episode as a "lover's quarrel" rather than a rape. There may be suspicion that the victim is exaggerating her claim of sexual assault out of revenge, or that she will simply drop her claim once she has had time to "cool down." This type of response—or lack of response—to a victim's report of rape can compound her recovery by adding to her anxiety, self-doubt, frustration, and distrust of the system. She now must contend not only with what her rapist did but also with the challenge of making the system work for her.

In addition, a victim usually receives strong support from family and friends if the rape was perpetrated by a stranger. Loyalties can be divided when the perpetrator is not a stranger and is known by family and friends. Victim credibility is especially likely to be called into question if the perpetrator is perceived to be a "good guy" and has a convincing argument against the idea that he would ever engage in nonconsensual sex. A victim of non-stranger rape also faces the possibility that others will have lingering suspicions that she was responsible for putting herself in a compromising situation. If a victim drank, was flirtatious, and agreed to be alone with a young man, others may think that "she should have known better." If she recounts what happened, the response may be, "Well, what did you expect?" Others may also wonder why she was not more forceful in resisting his advances. All these responses are forms of victim blaming.

If she was violated by someone she trusted, then she may begin to doubt her ability to judge another person's character. Perhaps worse, she may develop a generalized distrust of other men, including those worthy of her trust. This distrust can be immensely damaging, as our ability as humans to have deep, positive, and loving relationships relies on our capacity to trust others.

HOW YOU CAN HELP

There are several ways in which you can be supportive of a victim of non-stranger rape. Many of the recommendations provided earlier in this book can still be helpful, including the following:

- Even if police officers, school officials, or others express doubts about her credibility, reassure her that you do not have such doubts. It is important to remain steadfast in your support, regardless of what others may think.

- Let her know that even if she was friendly or flirtatious toward the perpetrator, she is not responsible in any way for the assault. Displays of friendship or affection do not make her liable for his actions.

- Remind her that the perpetrator most likely manipulated circumstances so he could control the situation in which she found herself. Non-stranger rape is largely an opportunistic crime in which the perpetrator could be anyone who is motivated to take advantage of another person's vulnerabilities, especially if that person trusts the perpetrator.

- The fact that her trust was used against her does not mean she is a poor judge of character. She needs to be reminded that the assailant is not representative of most males, and that other men can be worthy of earning her trust. In fact, your relationship with her should model the value of openness and trust.

- If the assailant is a family member, your first concern should be with the needs of the victim, regardless of the consequences for him. Neither her needs nor justice will be served if he is shielded from facing the consequences of his actions. As previously stated, outside intervention is required in this type of situation, which is understandably devastating to a family. Some family members may take sides, raising doubts about what happened or treating the sexual violation as if it were a mere dispute. The message you communicate in this matter should be clear and consistent: Addressing the assault honestly is not about taking sides, but rather about healing a wrong.

- Once again, do not let the fact that she consumed alcohol or drugs become the focus of your discussions with her about what happened. Her drinking or drug use was not the cause of the assault.

- If mutual friends or acquaintances remain on good terms with the perpetrator, you may feel betrayed by them. Assuming they know what happened, their continued acceptance of him most likely is rooted in his distorted account of what took place. Accept the fact that neither you nor the victim can control the perpetrator's narrative. Moreover, you cannot control what others think or say, nor should you try. What you can do, if appropriate, is simply reinforce your belief in what the victim has revealed about the assault. You may also raise the question, "Who has the greater motivation to lie: the victim or the perpetrator?"

- Do not be surprised if she expresses concern over what may happen to the perpetrator in the event of a campus disciplinary hearing or police involvement. She may feel somewhat responsible for "causing him so much trouble." Reinforce the view that he is responsible for his actions and that she did the right thing by reporting the assault. Her actions may save others from being assaulted by him. It is now the responsibility of others to determine the consequences he must face, and she is in no way to blame for his having to face them.

- If your daughter is a college student and she is the victim of sexual assault perpetrated by another student, school officials are obligated to keep information on your daughter's health and the circumstances surrounding the assault confidential. In addition, school officials cannot share information on the alleged perpetrator or specific details about actions they are taking regarding the investigation. You will only complicate matters for your daughter if you insist on interfering with campus proceedings. You should, however, read the school's policy on sexual assault, which should be available online.

- If your daughter feels the need to withdraw from school because of the assault, know that schools do not automatically reimburse tuition. She may also run the risk of failing her courses if she only partially completes course requirements. You may, however, petition the school's administration—typically the dean of students—for full tuition reimbursement and course withdrawal without assignment of grades. Sexual assault is a health and safety emergency, and the school has a responsibility not to add layers of stress on a student who has been sexually assaulted by refusing your petition. If the school is not receptive to your requests, civil litigation against the establishment may be possible.

- If there is a campus judicial proceeding or disciplinary hearing, make sure your daughter knows her rights and protections spelled out in the school's policy. Almost without exception, parents are not allowed to be present during such a hearing, demand answers to their questions, or interfere with the proceedings in any way. Under no circumstances should you contact the perpetrator or his family, or independently try to interview people who may serve as witnesses in the proceedings. The policy may also prohibit the presence of legal counsel at the hearing, as it is not a court of law. The most severe penalty a school can impose on a perpetrator is expulsion, not criminal sentencing. Regardless of the outcome of the campus hearing, the option of initiating a civil case against the perpetrator remains available.

- Unlike rape crisis centers, which emphasize victim advocacy, campus proceedings are concerned about due process and the rights of both the complainant and the defendant. Any student who is the victim of campus sexual assault should report it not only to school officials but also to a local rape crisis center. The victim advocate there can provide additional guidance and support beyond what the school can offer.

- Respect her decision whether or not she wishes to report what happened. Your focus should be on her needs rather than your understandable desire for justice.

CONCLUSION

Sexual assault most often involves people who know each other, with high school and college-age women experience the highest rate of sexual victimization. This form of sexual assault is known as non-stranger sexual assault. Typically, non-stranger sexual assault unfolds through a gradual series of interactions in which a perpetrator fosters his potential victim's trust and seeks an opportunistic moment to exploit her vulnerabilities. A perpetrator's strategies typically include the use of alcohol or drugs, and attempts to blur the lines of consent by invading his potential victim's personal space in a sexual manner. It is extremely common for a perpetrator to deny that sexual activity was nonconsensual. Victims often feel confused and responsible for what happened, which causes them to fear not being believed by others and reluctant to report the assault.

As a person who cares for the victim of sexual assault, the most important thing you can do is to communicate four fundamental messages to her. First, that you believe her and do not doubt her credibility. Second, that you do not believe she is responsible for what happened—i.e., that you know her actions did not cause the perpetrator to behave as he did. Third, that you do not accept the perpetrator's distorted narrative of what took place and neither should she. However much the perpetrator may try to gaslight her or others, she must know that you accept the truth of her account. Finally, that you will stand by her and respect whatever decision she makes regarding police or school involvement in the matter. An important step in her healing is her knowing that she has your support no matter what.

8.

Working with Law Enforcement

One of the most important decisions a victim of sexual assault must make is whether to report the crime to the police. A report will set in motion a cascade of legal procedures that will consume the time, energy, and the emotional resources of both the victim and her loved ones. For most, this legal process is stressful; for some, it is traumatic. The knowledge that working with law enforcement will be challenging—along with the widely held belief that involving the police and courts in the matter will likely not result in justice being served—tends to discourage victims of sexual assault from reporting. In addition, given the low rates of arrest and conviction of perpetrators, it is therefore a courageous act for any victim of sexual assault to step forward and engage law enforcement. This chapter offers guidance on navigating the chain of events that typically unfolds once a victim reports a sexual assault to the police.

Before examining what happens when a report is made, it is worth reviewing the many possible reasons why victims do not contact the police, some of which have been mentioned earlier in this book. A victim may:

- fear being blamed or not believed.

- feel shame, guilt, or embarrassment.

- be concerned for her reputation and fear public criticism.

- have had a prior intimate relationship with her assailant.

- want to protect her assailant from legal consequences, especially if he is a family member or friend.

- believe that there is nothing the police can do.

- have experienced negative interactions with the police in the past.

- lack witnesses who can corroborate her claim of sexual assault.

- fear reprisal directed at her, her family, or her friends by her assailant.

- not want to involve others who may have knowledge of what happened.

- not want to undergo a medical exam as part of evidence collection.

- not know whether the legal system would consider her assailant's actions a crime.

- fear that her drug or alcohol use would be revealed if a report were to be made.

- fear that her sexual history would be scrutinized if a report were to be made.

- blame herself for her assailant's actions.

- not know her rights and the protections afforded her in connection with reporting the assault to the police.

- not want to confront her assailant in court.

Victims of sexual assault may come forward and report the crime to the police for different reasons. Some may simply want to see their assailants punished, others may act primarily out of a sense of moral duty to protect other women from being assaulted by their attackers. Sometimes a victim's reluctance to report ends when she learns that her assailant has committed sexual assault again. It is important to note that the act of one victim coming forward usually strengthens the resolve of others to come forward as well.

A victim may also cooperate with law enforcement because people who know what happened—usually family or close friends—have convinced her of the value of doing so. Although it is inappropriate to pressure or coerce someone to report an assault, it is reasonable to make the case to a victim of sexual assault that reporting is a valuable option. If she decides to contact the police about the crime, it then becomes important for her to understand what may or may not unfold following her initial report.

WHAT TO EXPECT FOLLOWING A REPORT

If a sexual assault is recent, initial contact with police typically involves preliminary questioning followed by a request for a medical forensic exam. If a victim needs immediate medical attention, the preliminary interview can wait. The medical exam is a critical aspect of evidence collection and ideally conducted before a victim bathes, changes clothes, or even uses the bathroom. In other words, it is important that some evidence remain on her body, whether it the perpetrator's semen or another of his bodily fluids. Although she is a victim of sexual assault, her body is considered a crime scene in the collection of evidence. Often trained medical professionals such as sexual assault nurse examiners will use what is known as a "rape kit," which follows certain procedures for evidence collection and maintaining the integrity of the chain of custody of the evidence. A rape kit usually takes three or four hours to complete.

As mentioned, the medical exam, however necessary, can be terribly upsetting to a victim. Shortly after initial police questioning and the medical forensic exam, a detective will be assigned to the case and a more thorough interview will be conducted. Any statement given to law enforcement will be on the record. This questioning can be lengthy and emotionally draining. Remember, if the rape recently occurred, most likely she is still in the acute phase of trauma and could be experiencing disorientation, shock, fear, or other emotional extremes. The process of questioning could trigger flashbacks, which she will likely have no experience in managing, and she may not yet remember or feel able to discuss certain details of the assault.

However sensitive police officers may be in their questioning, this exercise may push her into an emotional space she does not wish to enter. She may even cease being helpful and simply wish to go home to avoid more questioning. She may also withhold information or mischaracterize certain elements of the assault, perhaps to maintain her composure. Her engaging in this type of behavior does not mean she is being deliberately uncooperative. Rather, it may be unrealistic to expect her to be able to provide a full, accurate, and detailed account of the event during the acute stage of trauma. As a result, she will need to undergo further questioning later and review her earlier statements. A victim is usually questioned on a number of occasions.

A victim will likely will be asked questions that she deems personal and confidential, which may include questions about the last time she had consensual sexual intercourse, whether she had any sexual involvement with the perpetrator prior to the assault, whether she consented to any sexual intimacy with the perpetrator prior to the assault and to what degree, whether she consumed alcohol or drugs prior to the assault, whether any of her friends witnessed the assault, and specific details of the perpetrator's sexual acts. It is easy to imagine how difficult it would be to discuss such personal matters with strangers. In addition, she may worry that the personal information she reveals in confidence during questioning will get back to her family and friends. This fear only heightens her stress and could affect how forthcoming she is with the police.

It is not surprising that many rape victims do not immediately contact the police. Days, weeks, months, and even years may pass before a victim decides to report what happened. Needless to say, any delay in reporting can hinder the successful collection of medical evidence. If you are a trusted friend or family member of a victim of sexual assault, you may be the first person to whom she speaks about what happened. If she decides to report the crime to the police, you will most likely be asked to provide investigators with a statement regarding what she told you and the circumstances under which this disclosure occurred. You may also be asked if you know or have had contact with the perpetrator. As a result, the victim may then feel responsible for dragging you into a situation that requires your cooperation with the police. It is important that you convey to her your support for her decision to report, and that assisting the police is not a burden to you, especially if doing so means bringing her assailant to justice.

One of the main objectives of police questioning is to determine if there is evidence of criminal offenses. The police will want to know whether the victim was threatened with or subjected to the use of force, coerced, incapacitated, or manipulated in any way. The standard for arrest is known as *probable cause.* Probable cause is based on two factors: 1) that there is sufficient evidence that a crime took place; 2) that the person to be arrested is more than likely the perpetrator of that crime. Most referrals to the prosecutor for arrest are rejected, and most arrests do not result in a trial or conviction. The district attorney plays a pivotal role in determining if a perpetrator should be arraigned (the formal filing of criminal charges by the state) and the case prosecuted. The district attorney's decision to go forward with a case usually rests on the following criteria: quality of evidence, seriousness of the crime, likelihood of conviction, and best use of resources available in the district. The simple truth is that sex crime investigations are resource intensive. One reason why they are very difficult to prosecute is that investigative units dealing with these crimes often are under-resourced.

Often law enforcement will seek additional evidence that the victim may possess to determine possible criminal conduct by the perpetrator, especially if the victim knows her assailant. Such evidence may include phone records, text messages, photographs, or other communications involving the perpetrator. Any post assault communications from the perpetrator could be especially relevant.

The perceived credibility of a victim also can influence the decision of the district attorney to pursue a case against an assailant. Unfortunately, there are certain victims who may not receive the commitment of law enforcement due to their apparent lack of credibility. For example, a sex worker who is the victim of rape may not be seen as a credible witness. Victims who are drug addicts, elderly or infirm, or disabled may also be seen as less than credible. Law enforcement may have a certain profile of what the ideal victim looks like, and if she does not fit this profile, some might think, "Who would ever want to rape someone like her?" Sadly, factors such as a victim's appearance and lifestyle can influence how claims of sexual assault are treated.

Even if a victim's account is believed by law enforcement, the district attorney still may decide against prosecution if the evidence is perceived to be weak or circumstantial. Most often the crime involves only the perpetrator and the victim, with no witnesses to corroborate the claim of rape, complicating whether to prosecute the case. Physical evidence such as DNA may or may not be available. Even if DNA is available, its presence alone may not prove sexual assault. The assailant can acknowledge that a sexual act occurred but was consensual. Failure to prosecute an assault, however, should not be seen as an indication of a false report or that the assault did not happen. If months or years have passed since the assault, there may not be sufficient evidence to move forward on the case. When a victim alters some details of what happened—a common occurrence—law enforcement may be more reluctant to advance her case. In addition, when some degree of consensual intimacy (or prior intercourse) between a victim and her assailant has taken place, especially if it occurred under the influence of alcohol or drugs, the district attorney may decide that the circumstances are not clear enough for a successful prosecution.

Civil Litigation

If a district attorney decides not to pursue a criminal case against an assailant, the victim still has a legal option: civil litigation. The standard of evidence necessary for a judgment against an assailant is much lower in a civil case. Criminal courts require the high standard of proof known as *beyond a reasonable doubt* for a conviction, whereas civil litigation requires only a *preponderance of the evidence* for a favorable judgment. In a civil case, as long as a victim is able to demonstrate that the event in question more than likely occurred, she will meet this lesser standard of proof. In addition, a unanimous jury verdict is not required for a victim to receive a judgment in her favor.

Civil law allows a victim to sue for damages such as medical costs, lost wages, interruption of education, and property loss. She also can sue third parties such as fraternities, businesses, or others who should have anticipated or done more to prevent what happened. Of course, successful civil litigation will not put a perpetrator in jail, and victims are responsible for securing their own legal representation. Nevertheless, civil litigation can result in a substantial monetary award and sends a message to perpetrators of sexual violence that there is a cost for their actions, even it this cost may not be incarceration.

If the police and district attorney agree that a crime was committed but the rape case is not strong, the assailant may be prosecuted on charges other than rape. Possession of stolen goods, simple assault, attempted rape, gross sexual imposition, importuning, or other crimes may form the basis of charges. If the offender is charged with what appears to be a lesser offense than rape, or plea bargains to a lesser charge, some may feel that the crime of rape is not being taken seriously. Some might see this lesser charge as a reason to doubt the victim's claim of rape. As a support person of a rape victim, you need to let her know that you take her claim seriously, that you know she is being forthright, and that her recovery from the assault is your first concern, regardless of the charges filed against her assailant. Quite simply, she should feel confident in your belief in her and know that your support is not contingent upon how law enforcement proceeds with her case.

GOING TO TRIAL

If charges are filed against an assailant, depending upon the laws in the victim's local jurisdiction, the victim may be asked to provide testimony in a preliminary hearing before a judge (or possibly a grand jury). The purpose of this testimony is to determine whether there is sufficient evidence to indict the accused. Very likely this will be the first time she will have to recount the assault under oath. Understandably, she may find the thought of doing so scary, but if she fails to appear in court for this preliminary hearing, charges against the perpetrator may be dropped. If the perpetrator is indicted, there will be an arraignment at which the perpetrator will plead guilty or not guilty. If a plea of "guilty" is submitted, a sentencing date will be set. If a plea of "not guilty" is submitted, a trial date is set, usually to take place in approximately three to nine months. The crime is now viewed as an action against the state, with the victim serving as the primary witness on behalf of the state. From her perspective, this lengthy and emotionally exhausting legal process may seem to depersonalize what to her was a profoundly personal and traumatic experience.

It is common for a victim to be apprehensive about testifying as her trial date approaches. This apprehensiveness may manifest itself in the victim as symptoms such as tension headaches, insomnia, loss of appetite, depression, nightmares, or generalized anxiety. The pretrial period can place great stress on her close relationships. Given the gravity of the situation, it would do no good to suggest that she not think about it. Such a suggestion would be dismissive of her feelings. Her anxiety is normal and understandable, especially in light of the fact that she most

likely has never had to speak in a courtroom under the cross examination of a defense attorney. Furthermore, like most people, she may have
only a vague understanding of the legal jargon associated with the case
or proper courtroom etiquette. As the trial date approaches, she may
express doubts about whether she is willing to endure the strain of this
process. It is therefore very important that she maintain regular contact
with the district attorney to receive updates and be aware of what is
expected of her as a witness.

Most jurisdictions have victim advocates available through victim
services. These advocates are trained to guide crime victims through
the trial process. They offer emotional support, inform victims of their
rights, help with victim compensation, aid in filling out legal forms,
and help in securing resources that support victims. A victim advocate
also provides guidance to a victim's family members, helps her to
develop safety plans, and assists her in preparation for the trial. In a
sense, a victim advocate serves as a buffer between the impersonal and
bureaucratic nature of the legal system and the emotional needs of a
victim who requires help in navigating that system. As a support person
of a sexual assault victim who has decided to prosecute her assailant,
suggest at the onset that she request a victim advocate to help her to get
through this extremely difficult experience.

Awaiting the trial date is likely to be a particularly stressful time
for the victim and those who care for her. Her assailant may post bond
and be allowed to live freely before the trial. She may fear running into
him or worry he will seek revenge while he is still free. She may wish
to file a restraining order against him in an attempt to prevent these
situations from occurring. If he, his family, or his friends try to contact
her or someone close to her, she should notify the district attorney
and her victim advocate. She is under no legal obligation, however,
to do so.

It is not uncommon for a defense attorney to deliberately employ
delay tactics to discourage a victim from pursuing a case. In fact, she
should expect a last-minute request to delay the trial, which may, in
fact, be an attempt to hinder the appearance of witnesses, who may
not be available at a later date due to their work schedules or childcare
responsibilities. Simply put: A shifting trial date may make it difficult
for people to testify.

Considering the degree of preparation involved in a victim's testimony, any delay in the trial will likely cause her great frustration. Moreover, the thought of having to place her life on hold and keep the assault at the forefront of her mind for a while longer may be emotionally exhausting. In other words, the longer the pretrial period, the longer she must wait to move on with her life.

Victim Compensation

One advantage of reporting an assault to law enforcement is that the victim may be eligible for financial compensation through what is known as the state's *victim compensation program*. Federal law requires all states to provide victims of sexual assault or other crimes with funds to cover crime-related expenses, which may include lost wages, medical costs, or mental health counseling costs. There are usually limits on each type of expense, but overall compensation may still amount to many thousands of dollars. Each state's victim compensation program has its own requirements and application form to fill out.

Reporting a crime outside a certain window of time can affect a victim's eligibility for compensation, although some states are more flexible with their time frames in connection with reports of sexual assault. Typically, victim compensation applies only after insurance has been used to cover whatever amount it might be of a victim's costs. Victims seeking compensation are required to provide documentation of expenses, such as medical bills or counseling fees. Eligibility in all states requires victim cooperation with law enforcement, even if no arrest is made or the case is not successfully prosecuted.

HOW YOU CAN HELP

Perhaps the best way to assist a sexual assault victim before the trial of her assailant is to help her to prepare for it. Once she knows what to expect at the trial, her anxiety in anticipation of it will likely diminish. Although no two cases are exactly alike, you can encourage a sexual assault victim to take certain steps prior to her appearance in court that may make her feel ready for the day and thus ease her fears.

- Perhaps with the help of a victim advocate, you should encourage her to request from the district attorney a copy of the signed statement she gave to the police when she reported the assault. It is important evidence, and reviewing it will refresh her memory of what happened. If there are discrepancies between this early statement and subsequent statements, the defense attorney may claim she is an unreliable witness who lacks credibility. She will need to explain any discrepancies and recall the detailed sequence of events when she gives her testimony. In a sense, preparing for trial is like preparing for an exam. Studying the material builds confidence and helps a person to avoid making mistakes.

- You may offer to accompany her to the scene of the crime, which may help her to clarify her memory of the assault. Provided she wishes to revisit the location, before doing so she should consult with the district attorney and a victim advocate on the matter. Do not pressure her; it should be her decision. If she does return to the location, it may also stimulate other recollections of the crime that may have escaped her.

- To familiarize her with the setting, you may offer to accompany her to the courtroom several days before the trial. Note the position of the witness stand and the jury box, as well as the direction in which she will be facing during her testimony. During the trial, if possible, you or her victim advocate could sit in public seating directly in her line of sight so she will have a friendly face to see in the audience as she testifies.

- As she will be required to describe under oath the details of what took place, she will need to know the appropriate terms to use when describing certain sex acts. The use of slang terms may diminish her credibility. With practice, she may become more accustomed to using the appropriate terms. You may help her to practice by offering to listen to her say these words.

- In consultation with a victim advocate, you may offer to help potential witnesses with transportation, childcare, or even lodging during the trial, if necessary.

- Remind her to request that she be consulted about any possible plea agreement in advance. The assailant may seek to avoid a trial by pleading guilty to a lesser charge. He may also wait until the last minute to do so. The victim may be happy to be able to spare herself the ordeal of a trial, but she may also feel that a plea agreement would be less than just. While the decision to accept a plea is made by the district attorney in consultation with the judge, the victim nevertheless deserves an explanation of this decision and a chance to influence aspects of the plea deal. One advantage of a plea bargain is that, unlike a trial conviction, it cannot be challenged on appeal.

- Suggest that she ask for a single prosecutor to be assigned to the case at her first meeting with the district attorney. This prosecutor should handle every aspect of the case—from the filing of charges through the completion of the trial or plea agreement. There are a few reasons why she should not want the case to be shuffled between several prosecutors. First, having a single prosecutor means she will not have to repeat the story each time a new person is assigned to the case. The trust she builds with one prosecutor can strengthen her resolve to go forward. Second, it takes time for a new prosecutor to be brought up to speed, which, in turn, could delay the trial date.

  Finally, the appearance of a new prosecutor may be seen by the defense as an opportunity to negotiate a more advantageous plea bargain or other deal. If the new prosecutor is less familiar with the case, the defense may try to exploit this weakness to get a better plea deal than the one offered by the previous prosecutor. Although it may not be possible to have the same prosecutor assigned to the case throughout, it may still be helpful for the victim to discourage the shuffling of prosecutors by stating the aforementioned concerns at the beginning of the process.

- Encourage her to consult with a victim advocate and the prosecuting attorney on how best to prepare for her testimony and cross examination. The defense attorney will try to undermine her credibility as a witness and perhaps imply that her conduct represented a misunderstanding between her and the accused. She should be prepared for the defense attorney to ask leading questions about her sexual behavior, her use of alcohol or drugs, how she communicated her lack of consent to the perpetrator, how some of her actions could be interpreted as her giving consent, and her motives for making such a serious claim to law enforcement.

She should know that nearly every state has passed what are called *rape shield laws*, which limit the ability of the defense to introduce an accuser's prior sexual behavior into testimony. It is important to note, however, that these laws do not apply to the accuser's prior sexual history with the accused. She should be prepared to defend her actions against the suggestion that she gave the perpetrator consent or bears a degree of responsibility for what happened. The defense attorney will seek to create doubt in the minds of jurors that her claim of sexual assault points to nothing more than a simple miscommunication between her and the accused.

• Suggest that she request from the district attorney a list of questions that are likely to be asked by the defense during cross examination. Under the guidance of a victim advocate and the prosecutor, and possibly with your help, she may wish to practice responses by recording them and listening to how she sounds. It will be helpful for her to learn to speak in a clear and deliberate manner. She may also wish to practice in front of a mirror. In addition, she should consider the clothes she will wear at the trial. Being properly dressed (no jeans or sneakers) can positively influence how she is viewed by the jury.

• Once the trial begins, the evidentiary information (including her testimony) will become part of the public record. Although her name may be withheld, some information about the case could appear in her local media. Recommend that she talk to a victim advocate about her right to confidentiality and how she may respond to information made public. If she is seeing a counselor, the emotional cost of public disclosure may be an important topic for her to discuss in therapy.

It can be extremely difficult for a victim of sexual assault to give testimony at the trial of her attacker, especially when the trial may be her first time seeing the face of her assailant since the rape. Furthermore, cross examination by the defense attorney may make her feel as though she is the one on trial rather than the accused. Your support and understanding before and during the trial can help her to avoid being traumatized by the courtroom experience. Your sustained support after the trial can help her to manage what comes next.

POST-TRIAL CONSIDERATIONS

A victim's connection to law enforcement may not necessarily end at the close of the trial. What comes next depends on the outcome of the trial and how the victim wishes to proceed in her relationship with law enforcement. If the jury reaches a verdict of "not guilty," the victim still has two legal options. First, as mentioned earlier in this chapter, she can pursue civil litigation and sue her assailant for damages. She will need to secure new legal counsel to do so, however, as the prosecuting attorney is now done with the case. Second, in consultation with a victim advocate and legal counsel, she can seek a restraining order against her assailant. A verdict of "not guilty" does not mean she doesn't have the right to be protected from unwanted contact from him.

If the jury reaches a verdict of "guilty," a separate sentencing hearing will be scheduled. If there is a negotiated plea agreement, the sentencing hearing is usually quick and relatively simple. If there is no plea agreement, the sentencing hearing typically involves the prosecution and defense making differing recommendations to the judge (juries do not determine sentences). The judge evaluates these arguments and determines the sentence based on maximum and minimum guidelines. Under federal law, victims have a right to be present at the sentencing hearing, though they are not required to be there.

Victims also have a right to be heard at the sentencing hearing in what is known as a *victim impact statement*. This statement can be either written, oral, or both, and is intended to describe the physical, emotional, and financial impacts the crime has had on the victim and others. The victim impact statement is submitted to the judge through the district attorney's office before sentencing. It is also made available to the defense attorney (and the defendant) and is not something that can be dismissed or subjected to cross examination. An oral statement, perhaps in conjunction with the written statement, may be presented at the sentencing hearing. The purpose of this statement is to allow the judge to consider the impact of the crime on the victim in the victim's own words in the rendering of the perpetrator's sentence. Creating and presenting an impact statement can be an empowering experience for a victim of sexual assault, as it lets her voice be heard and perhaps makes her feel as though she has some influence over her assailant's sentencing.

As a support person of a sexual assault victim, you can help her to prepare her victim impact statement. It can be an opportunity for her and you to reflect on the complex ways in which her life, your life, and the lives of others close to her have been affected by her assailant's actions. In a sense, the victim impact statement represents not only her voice but also the voices of all whose lives have been touched by this crime. This reflective process can be therapeutic, as it often leads victims to realize a newfound sense of strength. The feeling of having fought back, of having endured, of having some measure of justice prevail can form a powerful basis for continued healing.

There is an additional post-trial consideration that follows the conviction of an assailant: the perpetrator's eventual release from incarceration. In certain states, convicted felons may even appeal to the parole board for early release. Working through victim services, a victim has a right to be notified of a forthcoming parole board hearing involving her assailant. Furthermore, a victim can ask to have her victim impact statement presented to the parole board and request to deny her assailant an early release. Similarly, a victim has a right to be notified when her perpetrator is released from prison upon completion of his sentence.

Unfortunately, in most cases, the justice system does not automatically notify a victim of her assailant's release. In fact, most jurisdictions require crime victims to opt in to receive notification services, which should include notification of all relevant court proceedings and parole board hearings. These notifications are usually automated and may be sent via text message, email, phone, or letter. As a support person of a victim, remind her to check with victim services periodically to make sure she is still on the automated list to receive such alerts. You should also anticipate the release of her perpetrator to cause her anxiety over potential contact with him. She may also relive memories of the crime that she thought had faded into the background. If her assailant is out on parole, the terms of his parole will likely prohibit him from having any contact with her. She may wish to work with victim services to develop a safety plan should he violate the terms of his parole.

CONCLUSION

Whatever the limitations of law enforcement, it has come a long way in being more responsive to the needs of sexual assault survivors.

Positive developments include the creation of specialized police training, improvements in evidence collection, the establishment of victims' rights and victim services, and better access to rape crisis centers that work with the police. Nevertheless, it is not easy for a victim of sexual assault to endure the lengthy and complex legal processes associated with bringing a perpetrator to justice. Basically, in notifying law enforcement of the crime, she is also subjecting herself to additional emotional costs beyond those of her struggle to recover from the assault. These legal processes keep the assault in the forefront of her life, making it difficult for her to move on. In the end, however, her act of courage may result in two great rewards: her attacker being held accountable for his crime and her realizing that she is able to overcome great adversity.

9.

Rape as a Hate Crime

There is an unsettled debate among professionals in law enforcement and victim services regarding whether sexual violence against women—what some refer to as gender-based violence—should be labeled as a hate crime. A hate crime, or bias crime, is generally defined as a crime motivated by bias or prejudice based on the victim's race, religion, national origin, sexual orientation, gender identity, or disability. One of the most definitive characteristics of a hate crime is what is known as *victim interchangeability*. Fundamentally, this means that the violence is directed not only to the individual victim but also toward the category or group that the victim represents. The person is not attacked for what she has said or done, but because she is perceived to belong to a group that is devalued by the perpetrator. The characteristics of a person (e.g., race, sexual orientation, gender) can be crucial factors in her being targeted. It is a perpetrator's bias against these characteristics that motivates the attack. Quite simple, the perpetrator hates the type of person the victim represents to him, and the attack is meant to send a message of animosity and fear to that entire group.

It is true that each rape has distinctive features, and arguably not all forms of sexual assault will fit the definition of a hate crime. Nevertheless, some expressions of sexual violence require special consideration because of the unique challenges they pose to victims and their victim's loved ones. These cases include multiple perpetrator rape, interracial rape, and the sexual assault of a person who identifies as LGBTQIA+ or gender nonconforming, all of which fit the definition of a hate crime. Although there are significant gaps in our understanding of how victim recovery is affected by this particular type of sexual violence, this chapter offers a basic understanding of the dynamics and challenges associated with it.

MULTIPLE PERPETRATOR RAPE

Although most people refer to it as gang rape, sexual assault that involves two or more perpetrators who act together to rape the same victim is technically designated as *multiple perpetrator rape*, or *MPR*. Perhaps because most sexual assaults involve a single perpetrator, MPR has not received as much attention as other forms of rape—and the attention it has received has tended to come from sensationalistic media accounts rather than scientific research. Furthermore, official crime reports on rape do not distinguish between individual and multiple perpetrators, though estimates suggest that approximately 10 percent or more of sexual assaults involve more than one assailant. Consequently, little is known about the group dynamics of perpetrators involved in MPR, the interaction between these perpetrators and their victims, the process associated with target selection, or how the effects of MPR may differ from those of rape by one assailant.

What we do know, however, is that multiple perpetrator rape usually involves much higher levels of physical brutality, injury, and verbal degradation directed toward the victim than single perpetrator sexual assault. In addition, MPR often includes multiple forms of penetration (oral, anal, vaginal) during the incident and usually extends over a longer period of time than single perpetrator rape, with the victim suffering repeated assaults. Some victims lapse into unconsciousness during such a protracted attack.

Victims of multiple perpetrator rape are likely to have longer recovery periods than victims of single perpetrator rape. Many of them struggle with higher rates of PTSD and depression, and have a greater risk of self-harm after the attack. Victims of MPR tend also to experience low self-esteem after the attack, which is made worse if they perceive that others now see them as "unclean" or "contaminated."

Although the subject is beyond the scope of this book, it is important to note that one common context in which MPR occurs is during military combat. Invading soldiers have been known to use rape as an instrument of terror, torture, or revenge, knowing they are unlikely to be held accountable for their actions. In fact, unless there are strong norms and sanctions against rape within the military itself, rape of civilians on the opposing side of a conflict is seen almost as a right of the invaders—a spoil of war. Rape may even be encouraged by those in command as a tactic to demoralize and dehumanize the enemy. Unfortunately, victims of MPR associated with military conflict seldom receive treatment or legal redress. Although acts of sexual violence constitute a war crime, there is an absence of international enforcement mechanisms to prevent or mitigate this behavior. Perpetrators and those in command are almost never held to account.

What seems likely, however, is that some of the same group dynamics associated with war-related sexual assault may also be present during multiple perpetrator rape in nonmilitary contexts. For example, both military and nonmilitary multiple perpetrator rape is associated with young males who have a strong bond to one another. This bond is usually formed through their ties to a particular organization. In war-related MPR, the organization is the military. In MPR unrelated to war, the organization is typically a fraternity, sports team, club, or youth gang. Males in such groups often police each other's conduct to reinforce a narrow script of acceptable behavior and ensure conformity. In a desire to participate in male bonding, men in these organizations frequently feel pressure to make public displays of their power, bravado, and sexual prowess. For example, at parties thrown by fraternities or sports teams, members of these groups have been known to take advantage of individuals who are drunk, drugged, or otherwise unable to remove themselves from a particular situation. Often the victim is known to one of the group and perhaps willingly engages in some degree of sexual activity with this person, only to have other males take part without her consent and against her will. Most often the perpetrators will explain their actions as participation in group sex with a willing partner.

There are similar dynamics at play in youth gangs. Many male gang members have female friends or acquaintances who wish to become more involved in gang activities or are already quasi-members. These women may be required to go through an initiation in which, in the language of the gang, they are "sexed in." In other words, they are compelled to have sex with a member of the gang, regardless of their unwillingness to do so, to gain acceptance by the gang. Often they are coerced into having sex with multiple members of the gang. This initiation is usually facilitated by drugs or alcohol, with the victim being heavily under the influence during the rape. After the rape, she is essentially "owned" by the gang and likely to be subjected to additional acts of sexual assault in the future.

Perhaps the clearest evidence for categorizing multiple perpetrator rape as a hate crime is the sheer misogyny involved in the act. There is no doubt that MPR is a blatant expression of misogyny (i.e., hatred of, contempt for, or prejudice against women). Perpetrators of MPR see women as mere objects to be used and humiliated, existing only to serve the desires of men. As described earlier, MPR creates a powerful bond among the perpetrators of this crime, not only solidifying each assailant's sense of belonging to the group but also enhancing his sense of superiority over women. Some experts have described this phenomenon as a result of *hypermasculinity*, or exaggerated stereotypical male behavior.

In a hypermasculine group, male dominance over women is expected and functions to enhance group solidarity. The acts that took place during an assault become the stuff of legend among group members, who recount with pride to one another what they did. Often they will share cell phone photos or recordings of the event with another as proof of their "brotherhood." MPR can also serve as an obvious demonstration of heterosexuality. By engaging in this act, a group member is showing his fellow males that he is "manly" and not gay. The link between misogyny and homophobia here is quite clear.

A victim of multiple perpetrator rape will likely be concerned about her reputation. If her assailants are acquaintances, they may share the same social circle as her and present a distorted narrative about her to mutual friends. It is a near certainty that the perpetrators will try to shift responsibility for the incident away from themselves by claiming that "she wanted it" and consented to "party" with the group. The physical and emotional damage they inflicted upon her is made worse by their ability to fuel gossip and speculation about her character and presumed sexual proclivities. In addition, because what happened to her may have been recorded on cell phones, she will fear the recording becoming public. The recording could also be used as a form of blackmail to silence her.

In the aftermath of MPR, there is a question that may linger in the victim's thoughts and haunt her: Why did they do this to me? She may believe that something she did or something about her personality in particular set her up to be a target. You can help to ease her mind by letting her know that neither her character nor her actions were the

What Happens if the Rape Was Recorded and the Victim Seeks Legal Action?

A victim of multiple perpetrator rape may choose to report the crime to law enforcement and pursue a civil suit against the perpetrators (or the organization to which the perpetrators belong, such as a fraternity or a school's sports team). If photos or recordings of the attack exist, they can be used to identify the perpetrators and show what they did. The downside for many victims is that they will not have control over who will be able to view these photos or recordings. Judges, juries, investigators, expert witnesses, and defense teams will scrutinize this evidence. Even if there is a strong case against her assailants, a victim's understandable feelings of humiliation may be so deep that she does not want anyone to view such evidence. In addition, it is a near certainty that the defense teams for the perpetrators will interpret the evidence in a way that suggests she was a willing participant in "group sex"—an activity that they will allege happens often when young people throw "wild parties." Finally, she may not want to use this evidence because doing so would mean reviewing it herself and essentially reliving the attack.

As mentioned numerous times throughout this book, if you are the support person of a rape victim, do not pressure her to decide whether to move forward with the case. It should be her choice alone. Instead, discuss the implications of various courses of action with her and let her know that you will stand by whatever decision she makes. If she courageously decides to seek legal action, encourage her to consult an attorney about the potential risks of doing so and the existence of any legal safeguards meant to protect her and afford her control over who is granted access to recordings or photographs of the crime. Sometimes the best way to help is simply to listen to her concerns, acknowledge that her apprehensions about taking a legal course of action are understandable, and let her know that anyone in her position would have similar worries.

reason she was targeted. In relation to her rape, her individuality was less important than her being associated with a category of people—in this case, women—who are devalued by her assailants. Because people in this category are interchangeable as victims, and due to the collective misogyny of the perpetrators of this type of rape, any vulnerable female is an acceptable target. By helping her to understand the dynamics of male bonding and the demonstrations of male power associated with MPR, and by helping her to realize that nothing she did caused her to be a target, you will minimize the self-blame she may be experiencing. In addition, you should continue to convey to her the core messages discussed throughout this book: that you believe her, that you will stand by her, that you know she is not responsible for what the perpetrators did, and that she is not diminished in your eyes. These messages will form a solid basis for her recovery.

INTERRACIAL RAPE

There is surprisingly little information available on sexual assault involving persons of different races. Although most rapes occur between persons of the same race, when interracial rape transpires, it can bring to the forefront unresolved racial tensions and prejudices, which are an enduring aspect of our culture. Of the interracial rapes that are reported, most involve African American assailants and Caucasian victims. The key word here, however, is *reported*. There is solid evidence to suggest that African American, Hispanic, Asian, and Native American women who are victims are significantly less likely to report interracial rape than are Caucasian women. Distrust of the criminal justice system, fear of police, and concerns over possible negative responses by members of their communities regarding sexual assault by persons of a different race may all be contributing factors to the lower reporting rates among women of color.

Interracial rape fits the profile of a hate crime for several reasons. The victim tends to be targeted because of her race, which means there is a strong element of victim interchangeability associated with inter-racial rape. Furthermore, some cases of interracial rape also involve multiple perpetrators who deliberately select a victim of a different racial or ethnic group—a group they collectively hate. In addition, a perpetrator of interracial rape will often make derogatory references to his victim's race during an assault, further confirming the fact that racial bias was central to his choice of target. By using such language, the perpetrator wants the victim to know his racial motivation for the sexual assault. His goal is to demean not only her but all members of her racial or ethnic group. The rape sends a message of fear and hatred to the entire group, with the woman serving as both victim and messenger. Sexist language is frequently used alongside racist language, making it clear that gender bias and racial bias often work together as motivating factors when it comes to rape.

Perpetrators and victims are frequently strangers in cases of interracial rape. Weapons and threats of violence are commonly used to force victims to submit. As such, interracial rape evokes a strong sense of outrage in those close to the victim. Their reactions can include a generalized hostility toward the perpetrator's entire racial or ethnic group, which may lead to a dangerous yearning to act against that group, especially in the victim's male friends or relatives. If you or others constantly express strong feelings about the race or ethnic identity of the perpetrator, this may add to the victim's stress and her feeling of being seen as "damaged." If racial hostility becomes the focus of interactions between her and her loved ones after the attack, her recovery may be impeded. For example, if you or others close to her persist on prioritizing the perpetrator's race as a central concern, she may feel unable to talk about other aspects of the assault that are, in fact, more relevant to her recovery.

In addition, anger focused on the rapist's race may cause her to develop a generalized fear and distrust of all members of that race. Because daily routines often involve interracial contacts, fearful and distrustful reactions can be a serious impediment to her recovery and her ability to carry out normal routines. Furthermore, if she has friends who are of the same race as the perpetrator, these friendships could be jeopardized. Overemphasis on her assailant's race may result in her avoiding these friends, and therefore she could lose a portion of her support system. Equally important, friends who are of the same race as the perpetrator may prove to be invaluable in preventing the development of any racial hostility. Such friends also could serve as powerful examples of compassion and trust.

If you are a support person of a victim of interracial rape, you should:

- avoid making racial slurs and discourage others from making derogatory racial remarks. Such comments will only fuel her fears and may reduce her willingness to discuss what happened.

- emphasize the fact that most males of her assailant's race are trustworthy and would never sexually assault anyone.

- remind her that her close friends of the same race as her assailant still deserve her friendship and trust. If you notice her avoiding contact with these friends, suggest that she discuss this subject with a counselor.

- reassure her that you absolutely do not consider her to be "tainted" because she was assaulted by a person of a different race.

One tragic aspect of interracial rape goes beyond what it means for the individual who was victimized. It affects entire communities in a way that undermines the bonds that connect us as citizens. In some instances, victims of interracial rape choose not to divulge what happened out of fear that publicizing the incident could trigger open expressions of racial hostility or even violence.

Although the impact of interracial sexual assault on victim recovery is not well understood, there is no evidence to suggest that the recovery process will be more difficult than it would be had the perpetrator and victim been of the same race. Even if a rape appears to have been racially motivated, it is important for the victim to view what happened as an example of the intentional violence and degradation one human can impose on another, regardless of what the rapist's motivation might have been. The main point is that focusing on the rapist's race can prevent the victim from addressing her basic concerns: her feelings about what *that particular individual* did and how to feel in control of her life again.

LGBTQIA+ OR GENDER-NONCONFORMING RAPE

To better understand sexual violence directed toward people who are gender nonconforming or identify as LGBTQIA+, it is important to consider first these terms, which can be confusing. For clarity, *gender nonconforming* is a term used to describe people who do not express themselves in either of the traditional, binary gender roles of male and female. Some people prefer to use other terms to describe this category, such as gender fluid, nonbinary, pangender, agender, or genderqueer. Given the complexity of gender identity, this book discusses the concept of gender nonconformity in its broadest sense to include respectfully those whose expressions of gender reside outside traditional expectations.

The acronym *LGBTQIA+* stands for gay, lesbian, bisexual, transgender, queer, intersex, and asexual people collectively. The "+" is used to refer to those people who count themselves as part of this community but do not feel accurately represented by any of these descriptors. This book uses this acronym in reference to people whose sexual orientations would not be considered heteronormative, or adhering to the idea that the only normal and natural expression of sexuality is heterosexuality. It is important to note that this term does not refer to a monolithic group of people but rather a varied collection of individuals who identify themselves as being outside typical heteronormative boundaries. The concerns of this group can be diverse. For example, the concerns of a person who identifies as transgender may be very different from the concerns of a person who identifies as lesbian. Unfortunately, the common denominator within the LGBTQIA+ community is the fact that its members may become targets of sexual assault as a hate crime.

There is compelling evidence that people who do not conform to traditional gender roles or whose sexual orientation is other than strictly heterosexual experience much higher rates of violence than most other groups, including bullying, physical or verbal attacks, cyber abuse, destruction of property, sexual harassment, sexual abuse, and sexual assault. Gender-nonconforming and LGBTQIA+ individuals are among the most disparaged and harassed people. They also are disproportionately the targets of hate crimes, which may include rape. Despite the high rates of sexual assault associated with these communities, the rates at which these crimes are reported to law enforcement are quite low. There are many reasons why gender-nonconforming or LGBTQIA+ persons are reluctant to report such crimes. Many of these reasons are the same as those previously discussed in relation to cisgender (a term used to describe a person whose gender and birth sex correspond), heterosexual victims, but some reasons are unique to these communities, including the following:

- Fear of being "outed"—of having one's gender identity or sexual orientation made public.

- Fear that one's sexual identity will be mislabeled by law enforcement, medical professionals, or other professionals.

- If the perpetrator identifies as LGBTQIA+, the victim may fear being seen as disloyal or a "traitor" within the community if a report is made. Furthermore, the victim may also fear that reporting will reinforce negative stereotypes about the community.

- Fear of receiving homophobic (or transphobic) responses from law enforcement, medical staff, or other professionals, and of being denied legal protections or other services.

- Fear of having to educate naïve or uninformed professionals or service providers about LBGTQIA+ concerns. In other words, in a moment of crisis, a victim may be expected to help the helpers.

In addition to having these fears, gender-nonconforming or LGBTQIA+ individuals may mistakenly believe that sexual orientation or gender identity is an understandable—or even acceptable—reason to be targeted for sexual assault. The overwhelming theme that unites the majority of reasons for not engaging law enforcement, however, is fear—fear that seeking help will result in greater harm. From the perspective of marginalized people whose very lives are often stigmatized by conventional society, such fear is understandable. As a support person, it is important for you to acknowledge that these apprehensions have a foundation in reality and are not the result of the victim being paranoid or irrational.

As it is with multiple perpetrator rape and interracial rape, victim interchangeability is a defining characteristic of LGBTQIA+ or gender-nonconforming sexual assault. The individual victim represents an entire community that is perceived to violate cherished cultural norms and values. The attack, therefore, sends a message of hatred and fear to all who dare to challenge these norms and values. Any misogynistic or homophobic remarks directed toward the victim during the attack serve to reinforce the fact that it is a hate crime. They may also suggest the "corrective" nature of the assault—that it is intended to change or "fix" the victim's sexual orientation—which provides more evidence of the attack's true nature as a hate crime. In addition, a comparatively high percentage of assaults of LGBTQIA+ or gender-nonconforming individuals involve genital mutilation. Genital mutilation is especially likely with transgender victims of sexual assault.

Finally, overlapping of forms of discrimination demonstrate what social scientists refer to as *intersectionality*. The fact that persons of color who are gender nonconforming or identify as LGBTQIA+ are sexually assaulted at higher rates than other groups is an example of intersectionality. It also confirms that sexual assault as a hate crime may reflect a number of different biases.

Supporting Gender-Nonconforming or LGBTQIA+ Individuals

While the guidance offered throughout this book also applies to the support people of victims who are gender nonconforming or identify as LGBTQIA+, there are two additional pieces of advice that are specifically meant to help gender-nonconforming or LGBTQIA+ individuals who have been targets of rape as a hate crime. First, as a support person, you should let the victim know that a "gay panic" or "trans panic" defense argument from the perpetrator would be absolutely unacceptable and invalid. This type of defense is a form of victim blaming that suggests the assault was triggered by unwanted sexual advances made by the victim. Used to minimize or excuse the actions of a perpetrator by appealing to established prejudices against gender-nonconforming or LGBTQIA+ individuals, this bogus defense essentially characterizes the assault as a case of panic-induced temporary insanity. If this argument arises, let it be clear that the victim did nothing to prompt the attack or justify the perpetrator's actions.

The second piece of advice has to do with the fact that sexual assault as a hate crime can have a particularly harmful effect on how victims perceive themselves. The feelings of shame, guilt, and self-loathing that come from being stigmatized are made considerably worse when one is the object of hatred expressed through sexual violence. As a support person of a gender-nonconforming or LGBTQIA+ rape victim, one of the most important messages you can convey to this person is also one of the most simple: You accept who they are unconditionally, regardless of their gender identity or sexual orientation, and your acceptance of and affection for them are not diminished by the prejudices or misunderstandings of others.

CONCLUSION

Sexual assault associated with a bias against a particular group of people—whether this bias is in the form of misogyny, racism, homophobia, transphobia, etc.—conforms to the definition of a hate crime. Multiple perpetrator rape, interracial rape, and the rape of gender-nonconforming individuals or members of the LGBTQIA+ community are prominent examples of rape as a hate crime. Although there is still much to be learned about recovery from hate-motivated rape, there is every reason to believe that victims of this form of assault can find strength, resilience, and purpose with the support, acceptance, and devotion of those who love them. The hope and light at the end of the tunnel for every victim of sexual violence is evident in a phenomenon known as post-traumatic growth, which is the focus of the next chapter.

10.

Post-Traumatic Growth

Trauma can upend a person's life in ways both superficial and profound. Many philosophical, spiritual, and therapeutic traditions embrace the belief that people can grow in positive ways as they struggle with adversity. It is true that there is no magic spell to transform darkness into light, yet strength and wisdom can emerge as a person lives through and overcomes a terrible experience. With rape, the initial shock of physical and psychological trauma is often followed by a feeling of disconnection—from others, from one's sense of purpose, from one's sense of security, and even from oneself. But out of this grief and suffering a paradox can also arise. Many rape survivors report discovering hidden strengths and new insights as they fight to mend their emotional and psychological injuries. The struggle to overcome pain, including deep emotional pain, can enlarge one's sense of self and offer important life lessons. In other words, the paradox is this: Traumatic experiences can unexpectedly result in positive outcomes. Experts call this phenomenon *post-traumatic growth,* a term coined by researchers Tedeschi and Calhoun, who first put forth the idea that people can experience positive psychological changes as a result of their struggles with major life crises or traumatic events.

The concept of being healed suggests that an injury no longer significantly impairs a person's ability to function normally, but the process of healing is also a process of growing stronger in the places that were broken, and of learning unexpected things about oneself and others. Even though disorders such as PTSD can arise from a trauma, therapists note that this is not an automatic or inevitable outcome. They also note that stress and personal growth are not mutually exclusive. If negative stressors and the potential for growth exist side by side, then how can we shift the balance in favor of strength and healing?

Kintsugi

The ancient Japanese tradition of *kintsugi* offers a useful metaphor to understand post-traumatic growth. Kintsugi is called "the art of golden repair" because it is an art form that takes cracked and shattered pieces of pottery and puts them back together using a precious metal such as gold, silver, or platinum. The idea is to focus on the damaged aspects of an object and reframe the scars by calling attention to them as something beautiful rather than something to be hidden or dismissed. The scars now become a cherished element of the whole, adding strength and value to the object rather than diminishing it.

Kintsugi is a tangible acknowledgment that our lives include scars and other broken areas that can be made beautiful if we honor them by embracing the concepts of resilience and restoration. Post-traumatic growth may be understood as the art of healing, of embracing hope that the pieces of our fractured lives can be mended and revitalized in ways that add depth to our humanity. Post-traumatic growth reflects the idea that we can reframe hardships, that we have the capacity to rise above terrible circumstances, and that even the most difficult events in our lives can result in profound meaning, strength, and beauty.

Experts have pointed out different types of growth that often follow trauma. Each is an aspect of healing. Each involves a sense of realizing something positive that stands apart from one's experiences prior to the traumatic event. They include the following:

- Developing new interests, feeling greater appreciation for life, and finding a new direction or purpose for one's life.

- Feeling a greater sense of compassion for others who are suffering, especially for those who might have experienced similar trauma.

- Identifying family members and friends whom one can trust and rely on in times of difficulty, including developing stronger social connections with these individuals.

- Discovering inner strength, confidence, and greater self-reliance.

- Setting new priorities about what one wants and does not want.

- Maintaining commitment to achieving new goals and extending one's horizons.

- Finding new meaning in life, including a deeper connection to one's spiritual being or engagement with spiritual questions.

The concept of post-traumatic growth, however, is not meant to imply that trauma is a positive, worthwhile experience. It merely proposes that the difficult circumstances imposed on one's life can give it new meaning—that one may find light in the darkest of places. Post-traumatic growth indicates having traveled a path of reflection after a traumatic event on which one gained wisdom and purpose. Gaining wisdom and purpose depends upon one's willingness to engage in struggle without shying away from the introspection struggle demands. How is this possible? Among survivors of trauma who grew in positive ways from their experiences, is there a common denominator?

Although there is much to learn about the conditions that might facilitate post-traumatic growth, there is a noteworthy common element in the growth process among rape survivors. Growth is most likely to occur when a victim is assisted in constructing what experts call a *redemptive narrative*, which describes her traumatic experience and acknowledges the personal development she has experienced as a result of it. Even simply writing about what happened can help a victim to grow. Quite simply, for a woman who has been raped, the opportunity to tell her story and have others listen to it without judgment is critical to her healing. Relaying memories of a traumatic event allows one to reflect upon the motives and actions of those involved and offers a safe way to express deep emotions. The narrative, told in a loving context to someone who cares about her, creates distance from the event and allows her to draw inner strength from it. Constructing this narrative and sharing it with those who love her is a critical step in the growth that can occur for a victim of sexual assault.

SHAPING A REDEMPTIVE NARRATIVE

As humans, we tend to think about our place in the world, perceive our personal experiences, and make moral choices as if our lives are stories.

All of our life stories contain personal experiences that indicate something important about who we are. The stories we tell about ourselves fulfill a basic human need to connect with others and be understood. A person's redemptive narrative is a particular kind of story that progresses from a negative experience to a positive end. Experts who have studied trauma consider the redemptive narrative to be an important aspect of the personal growth process—of reflecting upon what one has learned and how one has changed in the face of adversity.

Ironically, however, little is said about the process by which one creates such a narrative, or the role others can play in helping a trauma survivor in this process. As someone who cares for a victim of sexual assault, you can help her to heal and grow by creating a safe space for her narrative to emerge. You can help her to be reflective and shape this narrative in a way that highlights positive outcomes. Whether she works on this narrative verbally or in writing, you can play a valuable role by asking her to think through a series of questions that will serve as markers for the journey she has been on and the kinds of changes that may yet come. In no way should these questions reflect judgment. Rather, they are intended to facilitate introspection and greater self-awareness. The following are examples of the kinds of questions that will help her think through what she has endured and form a redemptive narrative:

- If you think about the times before and after the assault, what are the main high points and low points for you?

- As a result of this experience, what did you learn about yourself that you had not realized before?

- As a result of this experience, what did you learn about others that you had not realized before?

- Did any of your relationships grow stronger because of this experience?

- Were any of your significant relationships harmed or diminished by this experience?

- Was there a turning point at which you felt things improve? Describe this realization.

- What aspects of your life do you appreciate more now that you have lived through this difficult time?

- After going through this experience, do you have certain strengths now that were not apparent before?

- Have you altered your priorities or goals now that you have gone through this experience?

- Have your values or beliefs changed because of this experience? How?

- Are there opportunities available to you now that perhaps you did not see before?

- Now that you have been through this ordeal, is there anything you wished you had done differently?

- Based on what you have learned, what advice would you offer a woman who is facing what you have faced?

- Based on what you have learned, what advice would you offer a male friend or family member of a woman who has been raped?

- If there is a central lesson from the journey you have been on, what would it be?

- What do you hope will be the next chapter of your life?

Your ability to ask thoughtful questions, listen but not direct her story, and express compassion without judgment can be true gifts to a victim of sexual assault. Such questions also provide an opportunity to reflect upon the journey *you* have been on with her as an ally, and as a man who cares about a woman who was raped. What narrative will *you* construct out of this experience? In what ways have *you* changed?

THE IMPORTANCE OF SEEKING HELP

While recovery can be an incredibly painful process for victims of rape, it is also important to acknowledge the heavy toll that being a support person of a rape victim can take on friends or family members. It often comes with emotional ups and downs, frustrations, uncertainties, sad moments, and even angry moments, all of which impact a support person's relationship with a victim. It is sure to include mistakes, missteps, and misunderstandings, as well as transformative moments in which both rape victim and support person find ways to overcome these difficulties and strengthen their bond. Given all the challenges associated with recovery from rape, it makes sense that, as a support person, you would need help and guidance yourself.

The good news is that there are multiple sources of help available to both sexual assault victims and their support persons in nearly every community. Rape crisis centers, community mental health centers, pastoral counseling, private therapists, and victim advocates are all examples. Unfortunately, many men mistakenly believe that rape crisis centers provide services only for women. Such a belief may be reinforced if local support services are referred to as "women's centers" and staffed almost exclusively by women. Men may operate under the mistaken impression that they will not receive a warm welcome if they go to such places to ask for guidance. The truth is that many rape crisis centers are open to men and run support groups for men who are striving to help a loved one to recover from sexual assault. Virtually all rape crisis centers will make referrals for men seeking additional help. There also are national hotlines and victim services available for free that offer helpful information and guidance. (See the Resources on page 145.)

Unfortunately, too many men have been taught to face their problems on their own, without help—to be "tough" and "suck it up"—especially when their problems make them feel emotionally vulnerable. The unfortunate truth is that many men find it difficult to acknowledge their emotional vulnerabilities and seek help. It is almost as if seeking help when experiencing something emotionally overwhelming would be an admission of weakness or personal failure—that it would somehow be "unmanly" to ask for assistance. Furthermore, many men are not well practiced in talking about their deepest feelings, fears, or emotional needs. They know that counseling, for example, will compel them to be open about their feelings—an act that is outside their comfort zone. Even if they do seek help, too often they stop attending counseling sessions after a few visits. Nevertheless, the simple truth is this: Seeking help from professionals places a man in a position to be maximumly effective in navigating the emotional labyrinth that is a relationship touched by sexual violence. Asking for help demonstrates a commitment to the relationship and is an act of courage.

As a support person, it is important for you to take care of yourself. Asking for help is part of self-care, of course, but it is not the only part.

Any online search will yield dozens of tips regarding self-care that are applicable virtually to everyone. Although too numerous to mention here, a brief list may include eating a healthy diet, regularly exercising, practicing mindfulness and meditation, exploring new interests, journaling, sleeping regularly, practicing gratitude, strengthening positive connections with others, engaging in leisure activities, setting new goals, and focusing on positive aspects of one's life. The point is that it is necessary for you to stay connected with your feelings and be mindful of your own wellbeing if you expect to help another person.

CONCLUSION

This chapter reflects a truth that is sometimes forgotten in the face of trauma, which is that terrible experiences can result in unexpectedly positive outcomes. Although there are no short cuts or miracle cures in the process of rape recovery, post-traumatic growth is possible for victims and the people who support them—including their male allies. The key to a rape victim's post-traumatic growth is her having a support network rooted in love and a willingness to listen to the story of her journey through adversity. Helping her shape this narrative, in fact, can be beneficial not only to her but also to you. Furthermore, by seeking help for yourself and engaging in self-care as you support your loved one, you will find that growth as the result of a terrible experience is possible for both her and you. Recovery from rape is a demanding journey. With your support, your loved one will find her way to this journey's end.

Conclusion

The goal of this book is to provide answers to a basic question: How can men help in a woman's recovery from rape? Most men in our culture have given so little thought to the impact of rape on women that when they find out a woman they know has been raped they become paralyzed by the fear of doing something that might make matters worse for her, or they react rashly and actually make matters worse despite having good intentions. The truth is that men can and should play a positive role as allies in a woman's recovery process. Although there is no single formula for how to be an effective ally, this book offers basic guidelines that men can follow as they endeavor to support women in their lives who are dealing with this difficult topic. The following points are essential for men to consider as they strive to help women recovering from sexual violence:

- **The starting point is empathy.** Place yourself in her position and try to see what this event and its aftermath look like from her vantage point. What might she be feeling about herself and others? How does she think others may interpret what happened? Does she fear being blamed? How might her world be changed because of the rape? What does she most need from you and others in the short term and in the long term? By trying to understand what she is experiencing, you will make better decisions regarding how you can help at each step of the recovery process.

- **Take your cues from her.** Do not try to make decisions for her or insist that she follow a particular course of action. The man or men who raped her also took away her sense of control over her own life. It would be counterproductive for another man—even one who loves her—to make her feel as though her life is not in her control again. In other words, resist the impulse to take charge. Your job is to play a more passive role by encouraging her to make decisions that will affect the course of her recovery. For example, it is not up to you to decide whether she should report the assault to the police or school officials, or in whom she can confide about what happened. Her need to regain control over her life by making decisions for herself is essential to her recovery. Your task as her ally is to affirm and support her decisions.

- **Avoid judging or blaming her.** A significant concern for most victims of rape is the possibility that others will blame them for the assault. A victim's use of drugs or alcohol, style of dress, friendliness, attendance at social gatherings, or other actions are not justifications for blaming her for the assault. To suggest that she is somehow responsible for what happened will only silence her and create distance between the two of you. The myth of victim-precipitated rape is just that—a myth. It serves only to blame victims unfairly and reduce the culpability of perpetrators.

- **Consistently communicate the fact that you believe her.** She may wonder if other people have doubts about what she has divulged regarding her rape. Very likely her narrative about what happened has gaps and inconsistencies—a normal occurrence—which may lead to skepticism in others. Repeated questioning of her "story," however, almost as if she is being interrogated, will likely convey a feeling of disbelief to her and should be avoided. If she believes that people doubt her, her willingness to seek help and share what she is experiencing will be undermined. Among the most important messages you can communicate is that you believe her.

- **Be patient and let her know you will stand by her.** Victims of rape recover best when they are not isolated and know that they have the support of others. One of the most important things you can do is to let her know that your support is steadfast and unconditional. Certainly there will be ups and downs in her struggle to come to terms with what happened. Nevertheless, your message should be both simple and profound: You will be an unfaltering and loving ally throughout her recovery process, no matter how long it takes.

- **Embrace the idea that her struggle will result in a positive outcome.** It is worth repeating that a traumatic event can, in the long run, result in personal growth. The support and understanding she encounters during her struggle to recover will form the foundation upon which her growth may occur. Never doubt that she will find strength in this crisis, and that your bond to one another will be stronger for going through her recovery together.

While this book is meant to teach men how to support women who have been sexually assaulted, anyone who wishes to be a positive ally to someone who has been raped or sexually attacked will find the guidelines given throughout this text to be invaluable. If there is a core to recovery from rape, it may be the need to work through the mental anguish caused by all the questions that arise in the wake of this intentionally violent act. How does one find meaning in the injustice of this act and the suffering that accompanies it? How does one make sense of the fact that sexual violence is so commonplace? How does one rise above the difficulties created by rape and turn trauma into personal triumph?

The truth about sexual violence toward women is that it compels a victim and her loved ones to embark on a difficult journey through emotional pain and uncertainty, with no shortcuts to be seen. Although the recovery process from rape takes time, in the end there is a better place waiting for her and those who love her, including the men in her life. No one can change what has happened. How one responds to the circumstances created by such a terrible event as rape is all that matters. In his book *Man's Search for Meaning*, Viktor Frankl offers a simple truth with profound implications as he states, "When we are no longer able to change a situation, we are challenged to change ourselves."

Resources

Nearly every community in the country provides rape crisis services, such as counseling, victim advocacy, or other forms of assistance to victims of sexual violence and their family members. For help at the local level, please do an online search using terms such as "rape hotline" or "sexual assault hotline" in combination with the name of your town, county, or state to find the appropriate resources available in your community. The following resources are national and international organizations that can be accessed online. Some include hotlines that allow callers to speak with professionals. Anyone seeking guidance in dealing with sexual violence should be able to find help by contacting one or more of these groups.

INTERNATIONAL

End Violence Against Women International (EVAWI)
Phone: 509-684-9800
Website: https://evawintl.org
End Violence Against Women International provides specialized training and resources to law enforcement so that it may better respond to victims. It offers survivors the tools they need to gather information and take action, making reporting violence to law enforcement easier. It also teaches a victim's loved ones how to respond when she tells them she has been hurt by sexual or domestic violence. Finally, it collaborates with other organizations to help victims, hold offenders accountable, and keep communities safe. Its website provides links to two especially helpful and highly recommended resources designed for victims and support people: Start by Believing (https://startbybelieving. org) and Seek Then Speak (https:// seekthenspeak.app).

UNITED STATES

American College of Obstetricians and Gynecologists (ACOG)

Phone: 800-673-8444

Website: www.acog.org

The American College of Obstetricians and Gynecologists is the premier professional membership organization for obstetrician–gynecologists. It produces practice guidelines for healthcare professionals and educational materials for patients, provides pregnancy and contraceptive information, facilitates programs and initiatives to improve women's health, and advocates for members and patients.

Centers for Disease Control and Prevention (CDC)

Phone: 800-232-4636

Website: www.cdc.gov

The CDC is a science-based and data-driven organization that offers schools and community centers a wide range of information on sexual violence education and prevention. It views gender-based violence as a national public health concern.

End Rape on Campus (EROC)

Phone: 202-908-5226, ext. 106

Website: www.endrapeoncampus. org

End Rape on Campus works to end campus sexual violence through direct support for survivors and their communities, prevention through education, and policy reform at the campus, local, state, and federal levels. Its website features a number of free hotlines that can offer support to those in need of help and answer their questions.

FORGE

Phone: 414-559-2123

Website: https://forge-forward.org

FORGE reduces the impact of trauma on transgender and nonbinary survivors and communities by empowering service providers, advocating for systems reform, and connecting survivors to healing possibilities. It provides training and resources to victim service providers and allied professionals on transgender and nonbinary survivors of crime and trauma.

LGBT National Help Center

Phone: 888-843-4564

Website: www.lgbthotline.org

The LGBT National Help Center serves the LGBTQIA+ community by providing free and confidential peer support, information, and local resources, including resources that address sexual violence. All support volunteers identify as part of the LGBTQIA+ family.

National Alliance to End Sexual Violence (NAESV)

Phone: 202-869-8520

Website: https:// endsexualviolence.org

The National Alliance to End Sexual Violence is the voice in Washington for 56 state and territorial sexual assault coalitions and 1,300 rape crisis centers working to end sexual violence and support survivors. It advocates for legislation to address sexual violence and maintains relationships with other national antiviolence organizations, including the National Sexual Violence Resource Center, the National Organization of Sisters of Color Ending Sexual Violence, the National Network to End Domestic Violence, and a number of others.

National Center for Victims of Crime (NCVRC)

Phone: 202-467-8700

Website: https://victimsofcrime. org

The National Center for Victims of Crime advocates for victims' rights in collaboration with local, state, and federal partners. It provides direct services such as attorney referrals, confidential helplines, training, and informational resources.

love is respect, National Dating Abuse Helpline

Phone: 866-331-9474

Website: www.loveisrespect.org

A project of the National Domestic Abuse Hotline, love is respect is a 24-hour resource specifically for teens and young adults between the ages of thirteen and twenty-six who are experiencing dating violence or relationship abuse. It is accessible via phone, text, or online chat and offers

real-time, one-on-one support from peer advocates trained to offer support, information, and advocacy to those who have questions about their romantic relationships, as well as to concerned friends, family members, teachers, counselors, or other service providers.

National Domestic Violence Hotline

Phone: 800-799-7233

Website: www.thehotline.org

This confidential and anonymous hotline provides crisis intervention, information, and referrals to victims of domestic violence. It also acts as a resource for domestic violence advocates, government officials, law enforcement agencies, and the public. It is accessible twenty-four hours a day, seven days a week, three hundred and sixty-five days a year, and serves as the only domestic violence hotline in the nation with access to more than 5,000 shelters and domestic violence programs across the United States, Puerto Rico, and the US Virgin Islands.

National Organization for Victim Assistance (NOVA)

Phone: 703-535-6682

Website: www.trynova.org

The National Organization for Victim Assistance provides professional training to victim advocates and crisis responders. It does not counsel victims of crime directly but rather connects them with the right national or local services and resources that can support their needs.

National Organization of Sisters of Color Ending Sexual Assault (SCESA)

Website: https://sisterslead.org

The National Organization of Sisters of Color Ending Sexual Assault provides culturally specific sexual assault prevention and intervention strategies, including technical assistance and training. It also advocates for policies to address violence against women that are informed by the experiences and meet the unique needs of women of color.

National Sexual Violence Resource Center (NSVRC)

Phone: 877-739-3895

Website: www.nsvrc.org

The National Sexual Violence Resource Center is a nonprofit organization that provides information and tools to individuals, communities, and service providers that can help them to prevent or respond to sexual violence. It uses research to determine the best practices to achieve real and lasting change. The NSVRC also maintains a directory of organizations that offer services to sexual assault survivors and works with the media to promote informed reporting on the subject of sexual violence.

Office for Victims of Crime, Department of Justice, Office of Justice Programs (OVC)

Phone: 800-851-3420

Website: https://ovc.ojp.gov

The Office for Victims of Crime is responsible for administering the Crime Victims Fund, which supports programs and services that are designed to help victims in the immediate aftermath of a crime and as they rebuild their lives. It invests millions of dollars each year in victim compensation services, raises awareness of victims' issues, promotes compliance with victims' rights laws, and provides assistance to service providers that support victims of crime.

Rape, Incest & Abuse National Network (RAINN)

Phone: 800-656-4673

Website: www.rainn.org

The Rape, Incest & Abuse National Network is the largest anti sexual violence organization in the United States. It operates a secure and anonymous 24/7 crisis intervention and referral telephone hotline service in English and Spanish. Services also are available online. It also provides information to individuals and community organizations.

Suicide and Crisis Lifeline

Phone: 988

Website: https://988lifeline.org

The Suicide and Crisis Lifeline is a 24/7 free and confidential support line for people in distress. It also offers prevention and crisis resources to people in suicidal or emotional crisis and their loved ones, as well as best practices for professionals.

VictimConnect Resource Center (VCRC)

Phone: 855-484-2846

Website: https://victimconnect.org

The VictimConnect Resource Center is a referral helpline that allows crime victims to learn about their rights and options in a confidential and compassionate manner. It is open on weekdays to all victims of crime in the United States and its territories via phone, online chat, or text. The information and referrals offered by this service have been made available in over two hundred languages.

AUSTRALIA

1800RESPECT

Phone: 1800 737 732

Website: www.1800respect.org.au

1800RESPECT is a counselling, information, and referral service for people who are dealing with sexual, domestic, or family violence in Australia. It puts callers in contact with trained counselors who can help them to identify what they can do and where they can find the right services or support for them. It is accessible to all Australians, including those who are vision impaired or hearing impaired, do not speak English, feel more comfortable communicating through a translator or interpreter, or cannot speak at all.

Lifeline

Phone: 13 11 14

Website: www.lifeline.org.au

Lifeline is a 24/7 crisis support and suicide prevention service for all Australians. It puts callers in touch with trained support people and is accessible via telephone, online chat, or text.

CANADA

Ending Violence Association of Canada (EVA Canada)

Website: https://endingviolencecanada.org

While it does not provide services directly to victims of violence, the Ending Violence Association of Canada provides individuals with a comprehensive list of rape crisis centers and crisis lines for every province in Canada. It also advocates for policies and resources to address gender-based violence at a national level.

WAVAW Rape Crisis Centre

Phone: 877-392-7583

Website: www.wavaw.ca

WAVAW offers intersectional feminist support to survivors of sexual violence. Its services take into account the needs of cis women, trans women, and people of all marginalized genders.

EUROPE

Rape Crisis Network Europe (RCNE)

Phone: +44 (0)141 331 4180

Website: www.rcne.com

The Rape Crisis Network Europe is an organization that provides European survivors of sexual violence with the information they need to get help. Its website is designed to help those who have experienced sexual violence, as well as those who are supporting victims of sexual violence, to find the support services available to them in their home countries.

UNITED KINGDOM

NHS

Phone: 111

Website: www.nhs.uk/
live-well/sexual-health/
help-after-rape-and-sexual-assault

The National Health Service offers information that can help people who have been sexually assaulted, whether they want to report the assault to the police or not. It allows them to find their closest sexual assault referral centres (SARC), which provide medical, practical, and emotional support to victims of sexual assault or abuse. It also lists other organizations and professionals that can provide help.

Rape Crisis England and Wales

Phone: 0808 500 2222

Website: https://rapecrisis.org.uk

Rape Crisis England & Wales provides specialist information and support to all those affected by rape, sexual assault, sexual harassment, and all other forms of sexual violence and abuse in England and Wales. It is also the membership organization for thirty-nine rape crisis centres.

Rape Crisis Northern Ireland

Phone: 0800 0246 991

Website: https://rapecrisisni.org.uk

Rape Crisis Northern Ireland is a nongovernmental service for anyone aged eighteen and over who has experienced rape or sexual assault in adulthood. It provides support to victims of sexual assault, their families and friends, and the wider community.

Rape Crisis Scotland

Phone: 08088 01 03 02

Website: www.rapecrisisscotland.
org.uk

Rape Crisis Scotland works with a network of seventeen independent local rape crisis centres and operates a national helpline that offers support and information to anyone affected by sexual violence. It also runs the National Advocacy Project, which is designed to provide guidance to anyone thinking of reporting a sexual assault as well as those already engaged in the justice system.

IRELAND

Dublin Rape Crisis Centre
Phone: 1 800 77 8888
Website: www.drcc.ie

The Dublin Rape Crisis Centre provides a range of services, including telephone counseling through the National 24-Hour Helpline and one-to-one counselling. It also advocates on behalf of survivors of sexual violence to help ensure that law enforcement officials, medical personnel, and the courts are responsive to their needs and act with sensitivity.

NEW ZEALAND

Victims Information, Ministry of Justice
Phone: 0800 650 654
Website: https://sexualviolence. victimsinfo.govt.nz

This website was developed by New Zealand's Ministry of Justice to help victims of sexual violence to navigate the court process after an arrest has been made. It also provides guidance to those who have experienced sexual violence on how to make informed choices about the actions they may take.

About the Author

Alan W. McEvoy, PhD, earned his doctorate in sociology from Western Michigan University. He is an emeritus professor at Northern Michigan University, where he served as head of the Department of Sociology and Anthropology. He is the author or coauthor of numerous works on rape, child abuse, intimate partner violence, toxic romantic relationships, youth suicide, and bullying. He has appeared on *The Oprah Winfrey Show, 20/20,* and many other national and regional television programs, and has also served as an expert witness in litigation involving violence in schools. He currently resides in Marquette, Michigan.

Index

B

Behavioral changes caused by
rape, 15–16

C

Civil litigation, 110
College campuses, consent on,
99
Communicating with others,
43, 45–47
Communicating with the victim,
37–43
Consequences
immediate, of rape, 19–35
for victims of non-stranger
rape, 100–101

D

Denial, accepting, 26
Dialog, beginning a, 37–43
Dissociation, 7

E

Emotional responses common to
rape, 52–56
Emotions and memory, effect of
rape on, 9–14

Expressing concerns, 23–24

F

Fear of retribution, 26
Flashbacks, 8, 67–69
Fugue state, 8

G

Gender-nonconforming rape,
128–132
Grooming, 81
Guidelines for mothers and
fathers, 83–90

H

Hate crime, rape as a, 121–132
Hypermasculinity, 124

I

Identifying signs of distress, 21–23
Interracial rape, 126–128
Intersectionality, 131
Isolation, 12–14

K

Kintsugi, 134
Kit, rape, 107

L

Law enforcement, working with, 105–119

Legal and medical procedures associated with, 28–32

LGBTQIA+ rape, 128–132

M

Male anger, 54–55

Medical and legal procedures associated with rape, 28–32

Memory and emotions, effect of rape on, 9–14

Men's role as support persons, 16–18

Multiple perpetrator rape (MPR), 122–124, 126

N

Non-stranger sexual assault, 93–104

P

Parental concerns during recovery, 81–91

Parents, guidelines for. *See* Guidelines for mothers and fathers.

Partners, intimate, guidelines for, 73–79

Physical injury, 66–67

Post-traumatic growth (PTG), 18, 59, 133–139

Post-traumatic stress disorder (PTSD), 8

symptoms of, 10

Pre-impact terror, 54

R

Rape

behavioral changes caused by, 15–16

common emotional responses to, 52–56

common sequence of events of, 96–98, 100

consequences for victims of non-stranger, 100–101

effect of, on emotions and memory, 9–14

gender-nonconforming, 128–132

grief, 60–64

as a hate crime, 121–132

immediate consequences of, 19–35

impact of, on sexual intimacy, 65–79

interracial, 126–128

kit, 107

LGBTQIA+, 128–132

long-term effects of, 51–64

medical and legal procedures associated with, 28–32

multiple perpetrator, 122–124, 126

psychological effects of, 7–9

questions in the aftermath of, 20

recording of, 125

shield laws, 116

trauma syndrome

acute stage of, 56–57

outward adjustment stage, 57–58

resolution stage, 59–60

Recording of rape, 125

Report, what to expect following a, 107–111

Responding to her disclosure, 32–34

Romantic involvement, future, 71–72

S

Self-harm, 25

Self-interrogation, 53

Sequence of events of rape, common, 96–98, 100

Sexual activity, risky, 70–71

Sexual assault, non-stranger. *See* Non-stranger sexual assault.

Sexual dysfunction, causes and forms of, 66–72

Sexual intimacy, impact of rape on, 65–79

Sexual violence, examples of, 14–15

Shield laws, rape, 116

Sibling sexual abuse, 88–89

Silent, why some victims remain, 30–31

Social media, 47–49

Spectatoring, 69–70

T

Trauma and confusion, 49–50

Trauma syndrome, rape
    acute stage of, 56–57
    outward adjustment stage, 57–58
    resolution stage, 59–60

Trial
    going to, 111–113
    post-, considerations, 117–118

V

Victim compensation program, 113

Victim credibility, 94–96

Victim impact statement, 117–118

Victim interchangeability, 121

Victim-precipitated rape, myth of, 44

W

What to do when she says nothing happened, 25–26

What to do when she tells you she has been raped, 26–28

What you should not say or do, 38–40

What you should say or do, 40–43

Untwisted

How to Use the Power of Love to Heal Your Emotional Pain

Ted Anders, PhD

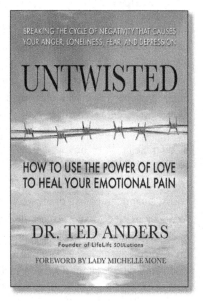

It's no secret that life can be hard. The emotional pain that comes with being human is often met with sadness, depression, loneliness, anger, or even rage. These reactions lead to more pain, and so a cycle of negativity is created. These days there is no shortage of pharmaceuticals being recommended to alleviate this type of suffering, but most of these drugs have potential side effects that could be worse than the problems themselves. And what's more, they address only the symptoms of emotional pain, not the pain itself. *Untwisted* offers a different perspective on the subject and presents a unique step-by-step approach to breaking this cycle for good.

Most of us go about our days under the delusion that happiness and fulfillment are feelings we need to search for in the outside world. This is twisted thinking. This book reveals that these concepts are not found beyond ourselves but rather lie within, and that we may achieve them by remembering a truth that has been with each and every one of us all along. Untwisted will guide you back to this truth and, in doing so, heal your emotional pain and bring you back to joy, your natural state.

Untwisted proposes a proven drug-free technique you can use to eliminate the root cause of your emotional wounds and transform your life for the better. By following the simple but powerful practices described in this book, you may begin to untangle yourself from the sadness, loneliness, depression, and anger that have had you feeling tied up for so long.

$16.95 • 112 pages • 6 x 9-inch paperback • Self-Help/Motivational & Inspirational
ISBN 978-0-7570-0453-7

Unexpected Recoveries

Seven Steps to Healing Body, Mind, and Soul When Serious Illness Strikes

Tom Monte

For more than three decades, Tom Monte has been a leading writer, teacher, and counselor within the natural healing community. As a national best-selling author, he has helped bring to the public's attention the work of many cutting-edge doctors, medical researchers, and scientists. As a teacher and counselor in the use of natural healing methods, he has worked with thousands of individuals and families who were seeking to overcome serious illnesses or other life-altering crises. During the course of his work, he has witnessed and written about many "miraculous" recoveries. As inscrutable as these recoveries may have seemed, Tom began to recognize common factors among those who overcame serious illness. Based on medical research, the insightful work of others, his own work, and the experiences of patients who managed to reverse their own devastating health conditions, Tom has written an inspiring guide for those who suffer from chronic or life-threatening illness. Unexpected Recoveries is the culmination of a lifetime of work designed to offer hope, purpose, and—most important—a proactive plan.

This book combines modern medical know-how, ancient healing practices, and a healing diet to provide a comprehensive and practical guidebook for physical, emotional, and spiritual recovery. It takes aim at such conditions as cancer, heart disease, kidney disease, chronic pain, Crohn's disease, degenerative bone conditions, and more. Readers are provided with a seven-step program to help them on their journey of healing, with each and every step designed to be flexible. Factors such as mental attitude, lifestyle, diet, and exercise are discussed in an informative and easy-to-read manner. Along this journey, readers are introduced to twelve people who have recovered from incurable illness. Also included are a helpful resource section, a twenty-one-day menu planner, and over sixty kitchen-tested recipes.

When a doctor tells a patient there is no cure, what the doctor is essentially saying is that there is no treatment proven to eliminate the condition. This doesn't mean that healing isn't possible. If you or a loved one is suffering from a severe illness, Unexpected Recoveries can be a powerful tool to change the course of that condition.

$17.95 • 256 pages • 6 x 9-inch paperback • Health & Fitness/Healing
ISBN 978-0-7570-0400-1